ASIAN-AMERICAN SCIENTISTS

ASIAN-AMERICAN SCIENTISTS

LISA YOUNT

Facts On File, Inc.

American Profiles: Asian-American Scientists

Facts On File, Inc.
132 West 31st Street
New York NY 10001

Library of Congress Cataloging-in-Publication Data

Yount, Lisa
     Asian-American scientists / Lisa Yount.
        p.   cm.—(American profiles)
     Includes bibliographical references and index.
     ISBN 0-8160-3756-6
     1. Asian American scientists—Biography—Juvenile literature. [1. Asian American scientists 2. Scientists. 3. Asian Americans—Biography.] I. Title. II. Series: American profiles (Facts on File, Inc.)
     Q141.Y678   1998
     509.2'273—dc21   98-10804

Facts On File books are available at special discounts when purchased in bulk quantities for businesses, associations, institutions or sales promotions. Please call our Special Sales Department in New York at 212/967-8800 or 800/322-8755.

You can find Facts On File on the World Wide Web at http://www.factsonfile.com

Text design by Cathy Rincon
Cover design by Matt Galemmo

Printed in the United States of America.

MP FOF 10 9 8 7 6 5 4 3

This book is printed on acid-free paper.

To all those

who build bridges

between worlds

Contents

Introduction

—————
—————

You are born, perhaps raised, in one country. Then, some time between babyhood and young adulthood, you move to another country halfway around the world. Its chief language and culture are completely different from your own. You must learn to get along in the new culture and add it to the old. Both cultures, and the task of blending them, are sure to affect your life.

All the scientists profiled in this book have had this experience. All were born or spent their early lives in Asia—India, China, or Japan—and then came to the United States. Connie Tom Noguchi moved while still a baby; Tsutomu Shimomura and David Ho came during their elementary school years. The rest immigrated as young adults to advance their education or scientific careers.

The ability to balance and blend two very different worlds shaped all these scientists' lives and, probably, their attitude toward science. Perhaps not surprisingly, this effect seems to have been strongest on those who made their move as children. Noguchi, exposed to a mixture of Chinese and American cultures from almost the beginning of her life, took part equally happily in the activities of both. By contrast, Shimomura, whose move from Japan came at about the time he entered kindergarten, says that he "never really felt that [he]

IX

fit in" with either Japanese or American culture. This may have helped to draw him toward the world of computers, which has its own culture.

Ho, who came from Taiwan when he was 12, also suffered temporarily from the change in cultures. Because he did not even know the English alphabet when he arrived in America, he says, "I remember being laughed at by classmates who thought I was dumb." Rather than discouraging him, however, this setback simply increased his desire to succeed. "People get to this new world, and they want to carve out their place in it," he has said. "The result is dedication and a higher level of work ethic. . . . You always retain a bit of an underdog mentality." His determination has served him well in the highly competitive field of AIDS research.

The scientists who came to the United States as adults have made fewer comments about their need to balance different cultures, but many brought elements of their Asian heritage into their new Western lives. When Subrahmanyan Chandrasekhar left India to do graduate work in England, he promised his father to "keep straight and be true to myself and, more than all, be worthy of the very fine cultural atmosphere which has surrounded me . . . from my childhood." He kept his promise by, for instance, maintaining all his life the vegetarian diet of his Hindu background. Tsung Dao Lee and Chen Ning Yang both decorate their homes with Chinese art, and Chien-shiung Wu has frequently worn the traditional Chinese dress called a cheongsam.

The result has been a cultural mixture of which these scientists are rightly proud. Yang wrote:

> I am . . . a product of both the Chinese and Western cultures, in harmony and in conflict. . . . I am as proud of my Chinese heritage . . . as I am devoted to modern science, a part of human civilization of Western origin, to which I have dedicated . . . my work.

A second-generation product of this blending, the older son of Connie Tom and her husband, Japanese-American doctor Phil Noguchi, has put the matter even more plainly: "I'm Chinese and Japanese and all American."

Having to build bridges between two cultural worlds may have helped the scientists in this book develop the flexibility and imagination to build bridges in their work, too. For instance, almost half the scientists work in molecular biology, a field in which researchers must combine the very different approaches of physics, chemistry, and biology. The scientists have also used flexibility and imagination to leap beyond known facts and predict the unexpected, as, for example, Samuel Ting did when he set out to find a subatomic particle that theory said should not exist.

One thing all these scientists share that can be traced at least partly to their Asian heritage is a high respect for education. Chandrasekhar's family were Brahmans, the highest caste (religious and social class) in India, and learning was strongly emphasized in both their Hindu tradition and the Western tradition they acquired from the British, who controlled the country in his youth. Har Gobind Khorana's parents were not Brahmans, but they were just as determined as Chandrasekhar's that their children should be educated. The Khoranas were practically the only family in their village who could read and write.

In several cases, the scientists' parents or other relatives introduced them to science in childhood. Yang's, Ting's, and Shimomura's parents were themselves scientists. Noguchi's and Ho's fathers were engineers. Chandrasekhar's uncle and boyhood hero was a Nobel Prize–winning physicist, and several of Noguchi's relatives, including some women, were also physicists. Chandrasekhar's, Wu's, and Noguchi's fathers filled their families' homes with books on science and other subjects. Ting's grandmother inspired him with stories about famous scientists.

Along with a drive toward education came an emphasis on self-discipline, precision, and achievement. Noguchi says that the Chinese culture's emphasis on "self-learning and personal excellence" shaped her life. Chandrasekhar's wife, Lalitha, commented on his "intense discipline about his work, an insistence that everything be neat and perfect," an attitude he probably learned from his equally perfectionist father. Wu, Ting, and Flossie Wong-Staal have become famous for the meticulous care with which they repeat and check their experiments. Ho's mother says that, as a boy, he "would be very upset with himself" if he got even one question wrong on a test.

The scientists in this book may also show their love of precision in their attraction to the physical sciences. Of the 12 scientists profiled here, seven (Chandrasekhar, Yang, Lee, Wu, Ting, Chu, and Shimomura) work or have worked in some branch of physics. Two of those in the life sciences, Noguchi and Ho, came there by way of physics. Noguchi changed from a premedical major in college to physics and then returned to medical research, while Ho started out in physics and switched to medicine. All of the biologists specialize in molecular biology, which involves chemistry and physics.

Discipline and precision are accompanied by a seemingly endless appetite for hard work. Chandrasekhar, Paul Chu, and Susumu Tonegawa often stayed in their labs seven days a week, sometimes until the small hours of the morning. Khorana once went 12 years without a vacation. Yang said that he "works even while sleeping," and Lee stated that for him "thinking is a continuous process." Wu once commented, "I have always felt that in physics, and probably in other endeavors, too, you must have total commitment. It is not just a job. It is a way of life."

An appreciation of the simplicity that lies behind the complexity of nature is a final characteristic that may have come from these scientists' Asian background. Such appreciation shows clearly in traditional Asian art and poetry, and at least three of the scientists have described it in themselves. Chen Ning Yang wrote:

> In the study of nature, one believes in something simple underlying all. The . . . simplicity and . . . beauty of the symmetries that . . . evolve from complex experiments are, for the physicists, great sources of encouragement.

More recently, Tsutomu Shimomura stated almost exactly the same idea:

> I became a scientist because I have always been fascinated with exploring and understanding complexity. . . . We have learned that what may seem a complicated phenomenon in nature almost always has a very elegant and simple explanation. . . . The search for elegant solutions has underscored much of my work.

And Subrahmanyan Chandrasekhar, at the end of his Nobel Prize acceptance speech, perhaps put it best of all:

> The simple is the seal of the true
> And beauty is the splendor of truth.

Wherever this almost artistic love of the simple truth and beauty of nature came from, it is obvious in the work of all these scientists. Science is the richer for it.

ASIAN-AMERICAN SCIENTISTS

Subrahmanyan Chandrasekhar changed astronomers' thinking about the lives and deaths of stars. (University of Chicago News Office)

Subrahmanyan Chandrasekhar

(1910–1995)

Imagine an object so heavy that its gravity sucks in everything around it as a bathtub drain sucks water. The object is invisible because not even light can escape its tremendous pull. Anything that falls inside this object vanishes forever into a universe that the human mind can hardly begin to grasp.

This strange object is called a black hole. It was once an ordinary star that died an extraordinary death, blowing most of its mass into space in a tremendous explosion. The star's immeasurably dense core, which became the black hole, was all that was left.

Such a dramatic ending to a star's life might seem impossible. Indeed, astronomers once were sure that it *was* impossible. When Indian-American astronomer, physicist, and mathematician Subrahmanyan Chandrasekhar insisted that stars larger than a certain size could not collapse and fade in the ordinary way, doubters almost destroyed his career. In the end, however, his theories paved the way for the discovery of black holes and many other advances in modern astronomy.

☆ ☆ ☆

Subrahmanyan Chandrasekhar—"Chandra" to almost everyone who knew him—was born in Lahore, in the northwestern part of the Indian subcontinent, on October 19, 1910. At that time, Lahore was a part of India, which was controlled by the British. Today the city belongs to Pakistan.

Education and science were an important part of Chandra's life from the beginning. His mother, Sitalakshmi, not only raised 10 children but translated literature into her native language, Tamil. C. S. Ayyar, his father, was an official of the government-controlled railroad and an expert on Indian classical music. Ayyar's younger brother, Chandrasekhara Venkata Raman, won the Nobel Prize in physics in 1930. Raman and Indian mathematician Srinivasa Ramanujan were Chandra's boyhood heroes.

Chandrasekhar's family moved to Madras, a large city in south-eastern India, when he was eight. His parents taught him at home until he was 11, after which he went to a public high school. He entered Presidency College, a part of Madras University, when he was only 15. People who knew him already called him a genius.

Chandra's father wanted him to study physics in college, hoping that Chandra would use his science degree to win a job in the British-controlled Indian Civil Service. Chandrasekhar, however, wanted a career in science itself, and he insisted on studying mathematics as well as physics. His mother supported his independence. "Do what you like," she told him. "Don't listen to him [your father]."

While Chandra was still an undergraduate, he wrote a paper on statistics that was published in the journal of Britain's top association of scientists, the Royal Society. On graduation he won a government scholarship to continue his studies at Cambridge, one of Britain's finest universities. Those studies focused on astronomy as well as mathematics and physics.

British astronomer Sir Arthur Eddington acted as Chandrasekhar's mentor but called his ideas about the deaths of large stars "absurd." (Yerkes Observatory)

SUBRAHMANYAN CHANDRASEKHAR

Nineteen-year-old Chandra sailed for England in the summer of 1930. Instead of partying like most of the other passengers on his ship, he spent the two-and-a-half-week journey staring at the sky and thinking. Astronomers at the time believed that all stars ended their lives as immensely heavy planet-sized cinders called white dwarfs. Chandrasekhar, however, did not think that the white dwarf theory took into account the effects of relativity, the world-shaking theory proposed by Swiss mathematician Albert Einstein. During the voyage, Chandra began to calculate the effect that relativity should have on the gravity of stars with different masses. He continued this work in Cambridge, earning his Ph.D. in 1933.

Chandrasekhar's mathematics led him to some startling conclusions. He decided that for stars with masses up to 1.44 times that of the sun—a group that included most stars—the white dwarf theory was right. The tremendous gravity of larger stars, however, would force them to go on shrinking below white dwarf size. Indeed, they might never stop.

Chandrasekhar often talked over his ideas with renowned astronomer Sir Arthur Eddington, who had helped to establish the white dwarf theory. Eddington did not say exactly what he thought of Chandra's ideas, but he seemed to support his young colleague's work. He acted as Chandra's mentor and friend.

Chandra read a paper describing his theory at a meeting of the Royal Astronomical Society on January 11, 1935. His audience seemed to receive his work well in spite of its unusual ideas. But then, to Chandra's amazement, Arthur Eddington rose to speak. He could find no fault with Chandrasekhar's mathematics or logic, Eddington said, but one of Chandra's fundamental assumptions must be wrong, since it had led him to such ridiculous conclusions. According to Chandra's prediction, Eddington noted sarcastically,

> The star [with mass greater than 1.44 times that of the sun] has to go on radiating and radiating and contracting and contracting until, I suppose, it gets to a few km. [kilometers] radius, when gravity becomes strong enough to hold in the radiation, and the star can at last find peace. . . . I think there should be a law of Nature to prevent a star from behaving in this absurd way!

Chandrasekhar was devastated. He couldn't understand how a man he had thought was his friend could turn on him like this. If Eddington had doubted his work, why had he not told Chandra privately rather than making a fool of him in public? Worse still, Chandra knew that Eddington's opinions carried enormous weight. If Eddington said he was wrong, most other astronomers would agree without question. Late that night, after returning to Cambridge, Chandra stared into the fire in the faculty common room, thinking of the last lines of a famous poem by T. S. Eliot: "This is the way the world ends/Not with a bang but a whimper."

Chandra sent his work to several prominent physicists and asked for their opinion of it. They reassured him privately that they thought he was right, but they would not make their support public. The result was that, as Chandra had predicted, Eddington's view held sway among astronomers for more than 20 years.

Amazingly, Chandra held no grudge against Eddington. He even said long afterward that, in the long run, it may have been better for him that Eddington did not support him. He thought his apparent failure might have kept him from developing "a certain arrogance toward nature" that had limited the work of some scientists who became famous at an early age.

At the time, however, Chandrasekhar knew only that Eddington's disapproval of his ideas would make a career in England almost impossible. He did not want to work in India, either, where scientific appointments were closely intertwined with politics. He returned there in 1936 only long enough to see his family and marry Lalitha Doraiswamy, a young woman whom he had first met in his physics classes at Presidency College.

Astronomer Otto Struve offered Chandrasekhar a position at the University of Chicago's Yerkes Observatory in Williams Bay, Wisconsin, and Chandra accepted. He and Lalitha moved to the United States in 1937. Until 1963 he worked mostly at the observatory, which was about 100 miles from the university. After that he became a professor at the university, where he remained until his death.

Chandrasekhar's way of working puzzled many of his fellow professors. He would bury himself in a subject for eight or ten years and then finally, when he felt that he could see it "as a whole with a perspective," write a book on it. After that he would change to a completely different area of research. He once said, "If you make a sculpture, you finish it—you don't want to go on chipping it here and there."

For instance, although Chandra continued to believe that his ideas about the ways stars died were right, he abandoned this subject two years after coming to Yerkes. First, however, he wrote a book on it, titled *An Introduction to the Study of Stellar Structure.* Like most of his later books, this one remained a standard reference work for decades.

Chandra turned to a different astronomical problem, the study of star clusters, in the early 1940s. He found that the gravity of these stars, which were packed relatively close together, slowed the stars' movement as they passed each other. This affected the way the clusters changed over time.

World War II was raging at this time. To help the war effort, Chandrasekhar became a consultant for the Ballistic Research Laboratory at the Aberdeen Proving Ground in Maryland. He helped scientists there determine how gases behaved during explosions such as the firing of a gun.

At Aberdeen, unfortunately, Chandra encountered some of the racial prejudice that African Americans had to endure. One day, for instance, he tried to enter the grounds through a gate manned by a soldier who did not recognize him. The soldier shouted, "Eh blackie, you just wait until I come!" and left him standing there for an hour.

After the war, Chandrasekhar investigated the way energy is transferred through radiation inside stars. Then, in the 1950s, he studied the fluid movements and magnetic fields of the chaotic soup of electrically charged particles called plasma. He concluded that many galaxies, including Earth's own Milky Way, are surrounded by magnetic fields so intense that they deform some of the stars inside. During the 1960s, he worked out mathematical rules for the behavior of shapes called ellipsoids. These shapes do not exist in nature, but later scientists found that Chandra's rules helped them understand what holds spinning galaxies together.

By the 1970s, Chandrasekhar had reached an age where most scientists would think of retiring. He had a heart attack, followed by open heart surgery, in 1975. Instead of stopping his work, however, Chandra returned to his first love, the life cycles and deaths of stars. He did research on black holes, mysterious objects whose existence was first suspected because of his pioneering work at Cambridge.

Other scientists had long since shown that Chandrasekhar, not Eddington, had been right: Stars with masses over what came to be known as the Chandrasekhar limit ended their lives differently than smaller stars did. They tore themselves apart in immense explosions, becoming what are known as supernovas. Afterward their cores shrank down to extremely small, dense bodies called neutron stars. A cup of matter from a neutron star weighs more than Mount Everest.

There is a secret society whose activities transcend all limits in space and time, and Dr. Chandrasekhar is one of its members. It is the ideal community of geniuses who weave . . . our culture.

—Res Jost, on awarding Chandrasekhar the Tamala Prize in 1984

Furthermore, just as Chandra had predicted, some stars apparently shrink even beyond that. Building on Chandrasekhar's calculations, scientists such as British astrophysicist Stephen Hawking showed mathematically that such stars eventually become black holes. Indirect evidence has now convinced most astronomers that black holes actually exist. Huge black holes seem to sit in the centers of many galaxies, including Earth's own.

While Chandrasekhar was adding to the work that he had done so long ago, he won science's ultimate prize for that work. On his birthday in 1983, at the age of 73, he was given the Nobel Prize in physics for his studies of the deaths of stars. He did not seem upset that the award had come some 50 years after the research it honored. "Usually my work has become appreciated only after some length of time," he remarked.

Chandrasekhar showed that stars with a mass greater than 1.44 times that of the sun die in a violent explosion, becoming what are called supernovas. The Crab Nebula, shown here, is a cloud of glowing gas left from a supernova explosion that took place in A.D.1054 and was visible from the Earth. The tiny, unbelievably dense remains of the star are hidden inside the cloud. (Yerkes Observatory)

The Nobel Prize was the greatest honor given to Chandrasekhar, but it was far from the only one. Others included the Royal Astronomical Society's Gold Medal (1953), the Draper Award of the U.S. National Academy of Sciences (1968), and the Padma Vibushan award from the government of India. He also received the Rumford Medal of the American Academy of Arts and Sciences (1957), the Royal Medal of Britain's Royal Society (1962), and the National Science Medal.

Because of his intense devotion to science, Chandrasekhar once said, "I had to sacrifice other interests in life—literature, music, traveling. I wanted to read all the plays of Shakespeare very carefully, line by line, word by word. I have never found the time to do it." He did not give up these interests completely, however. He was always fond of the best of English literature and of classical composers such as Bach and Beethoven.

Chandrasekhar also found time to be an inspiring teacher and to personally encourage the most brilliant of his students. One year he had a class consisting only of two young men from China, Tsung Dao Lee and Chen Ning Yang. During the winter, he drove across a hundred miles of icy roads between Williams Bay and Chicago just to meet with them. Like Chandrasekhar, these young men went on to win a Nobel Prize.

Chandrasekhar's last book was devoted to explaining the *Principia Mathematica*, the chief work of the great 17th-century scientist Isaac Newton. Chandra called Newton "one of the two or three greatest intellects, ever, in any subject." Uncharacteristically, he made no plans about what he would do after he finished the book on Newton. "That's the end," he told *Scientific American* interviewer John Horgan in 1994. His words were prophetic. Subrahmanyan Chandrasekhar died on August 21, 1995, just two months after his book was completed.

Writing Chandra's obituary in the magazine *Physics Today*, Eugene N.

T*he simple is the seal of the true, and beauty is the splendor of truth.*

—Subrahmanyan Chandrasekhar, at conclusion of his Nobel Prize acceptance speech

Parker of the University of Chicago said that his death "marks the passing of an era in which physicists first reached inward to understand the atom and the fundamental particles [inside it] and outward to embrace the stars." Physicist Philip Morrison of the Massachusetts Institute of Technology (MIT) has added that Chandrasekhar's "mathematical insight and . . . elegance has been responsible for most of what we know about stars."

Chronology

OCTOBER 19, 1910	Subrahmanyan Chandrasekhar born in Lahore, India
1929	paper on statistics published in Britain
1930	Chandrasekhar begins study at Cambridge University in England; proposes theory of how large stars die
1933	earns Ph.D. in astrophysics from Cambridge
JANUARY 11, 1935	presents paper to Royal Astronomical Society
1937	joins University of Chicago's Yerkes Observatory
1939	publishes book on structure of stars
EARLY 1940S	studies star clusters; acts as consultant at Aberdeen Proving Ground
LATE 1940S	studies radiation inside stars
1950S	studies movements and magnetic fields in plasma
1960S	studies ellipsoids
1970S	studies black holes

OCTOBER 19, 1983	is awarded Nobel Prize in physics
LATE 1980S	studies Isaac Newton's *Principia Mathematica*
AUGUST 21, 1995	Chandrasekhar dies

Further Reading

"Chandrasekhar, Subrahmanyan." *Current Biography 1986.* New York: H.W. Wilson, 1986. Brief but information-packed biographical sketch.

Horgan, John. "Confronting the Final Limit." *Scientific American,* March 1994, pp. 32–33. Interview with Chandrasekhar near the end of his life.

Parker, Eugene N. "Subrahmanyan Chandrasekhar." *Physics Today,* November 1995, pp. 106–108. Obituary/biographical sketch.

Ragaza, Angelo. *Lives of Notable Asian Americans.* New York: Chelsea House, 1995. For young adults. Includes good chapter on Chandrasekhar.

Tierney, John. "Quest for Order." In Allen L. Hammond, ed., *A Passion to Know.* New York: Scribner, 1984. Interview and biographical profile.

Wali, Kameshwar C. *Chandra.* Chicago: University of Chicago Press, 1991. Book-length biography of Chandrasekhar.

Chien-Shiung Wu
Chen Ning Yang
Tsung Dao Lee

(1912–)
(1922–)
(1926–)

Suppose you wake up one morning and see the sun slowly rising—out of the west. You find yourself walking on the ceiling of your home because the force of gravity is pulling things up instead of down. How do you feel?

Physicists felt almost that shaken up in January 1957 when they learned that three Chinese Americans had done what seemed just as impossible as reversing the rotation of the Earth or the law of gravity. The theory of Chen Ning Yang and Tsung Dao Lee, tested in an

Tsung Dao Lee, left, and Chen Ning Yang, right, disproved what had been thought to be a basic law of physics. (photo Alan W. Richards; American Institute of Physics, Emilio Segrè Visual Archives)

elegant experiment by Chien-shiung Wu, had disproved a rule called the conservation of parity, which had been thought to be a basic law of physics.

Chen Ning Yang, the older of the two men who decided to question this fundamental law, was born on September 22, 1922, in Hofei, northern China. The oldest of five children, he grew up in the quiet atmosphere of Tsinghua University in Beijing, the Chinese capital. His father, Meng-hua Yang, was a mathematics professor there.

By the time Yang himself was ready for college, the quiet times were over. Japan invaded northern China, starting with the area around Beijing, in 1937. To avoid the war, Yang went south to

Kunming and took his university training at National Southwest Associated University. He received his B.S. in 1942 and remained at the university for graduate work.

While at the university, Yang met another physics student, Tsung Dao Lee, who was four years younger than himself. Lee had been born on November 24, 1926, in Shanghai. He was the third child of a businessman, Tsing-kong Lee, and his wife, Ming-chang. He came to National Southwest Associated University in 1945.

Yang won a scholarship to do graduate work in the United States. He arrived at the University of Chicago in 1945. Eager to adapt to his new country, he began calling himself Franklin, or Frank, after Benjamin Franklin, whom he greatly admired. Within a few months, Lee, still an undergraduate, came to the same university as an assistant to a Chinese physics professor. Yang and Lee had not known each other well in China, but in Chicago they became coworkers and close friends.

At the university, the two young men had their choice of world-famous physics professors, including Enrico Fermi and Edward Teller, who had helped to develop the atomic bomb. Yang studied atomic physics with Teller, while Lee did research under Fermi on the hydrogen in white dwarf stars. Both men also took a special class from Subrahmanyan Chandrasekhar, in which they were the only students. Yang received his Ph.D. in 1948 and Lee in 1950.

Yang and Lee, like Chandrasekhar, were theorists rather than experimenters. Their greatest interest was in the strange world inside the atom. When they began their careers, knowledge of that world was exploding as fiercely as uranium atoms inside an atomic bomb. Physicists in the 1930s had thought there were only three kinds of particles inside atoms: protons, electrons, and neutrons. After the war, however,

T*he theoretists [scientists who form theories] . . . serve as an intermediary between the experimentalists and the final goal of all physics. That goal is synthesis, the simple plan.*

—Chen Ning Yang

scientists built giant machines called cyclotrons, which smashed atoms into tiny fragments. The cyclotrons revealed dozens of new subatomic particles, many of which existed for only a fraction of a second before breaking down into energy or other particles.

Yang and Lee split up for a while after Yang completed his studies at the University of Chicago, though they kept in touch by letter. Yang went to the Institute for Advanced Study, a part of Princeton University in New Jersey, in 1949. There he met a young woman named Chih-li Tu, whom he had first known in China when he taught mathematics at her high school. Their reacquaintance led to marriage on August 26, 1950. They went on to have two sons and a daughter. Lee, still in Chicago finishing his Ph.D., had also married just a few months earlier. His bride was Jeannette Hui-chung Chin, a young woman he had met at the university. They later had two sons.

Soon after he completed his doctorate, Lee went to the University of California at Berkeley, home of one of the country's two largest cyclotrons. A year later he joined Yang at Princeton, where he remained until 1953. He then moved on to Columbia University in New York City. He became Columbia's youngest full professor in January 1956, just two months after his 29th birthday.

Princeton and Columbia were not far apart, and Lee and Yang often got together for lunch. In the spring of 1956, one topic they discussed was a problem called the tau-theta puzzle, which concerned two recently discovered subatomic particles belonging to a group called K mesons. One particle, named tau after the 19th letter of the Greek alphabet, decayed or broke down into three other particles called pi mesons or pions. The other, the theta particle (theta is the eighth Greek letter), broke down into two pions. In all other ways, such as mass and electric charge, the tau and theta mesons were exactly alike. They would have been considered to be the same particle except for their different decay behavior. A single kind of particle that decayed in two different ways would violate what physicists assumed to be a basic law of matter: the law of conservation of parity.

This law said that any physical object or system and its mirror image will obey the same laws of physics. In other words, most humans may be either right-handed or left-handed, but nature is not. All subatomic particles have mirror-image equivalents, and because of the parity law, physicists assumed that each particle and its mirror opposite behaved exactly alike. First formulated in 1927, the parity law had been proved true for most kinds of actions both inside and outside the atom. It was as widely accepted as, say, the law of gravity.

Yang wrote later that the situation of physicists thinking about the tau-theta puzzle was like "a man in a dark room groping for an outlet [exit]. He is aware of the fact that in some direction there must be a door which would lead him out of his predicament. But in which direction?"

The first person to suggest a possible direction was Richard Feynman, a physicist from the California Institute of Technology (Caltech). At a physics conference in April 1956 that Yang and Lee attended, Feynman pointed out that the different decays of tau and theta could be explained quite simply if the law of conservation of parity did not hold true for the class of subatomic behaviors called weak interactions. Particle decay was one kind of weak interaction. If the parity law did not apply to such interactions, the same particle could decay differently in its right-handed form than it did in its left-handed form.

Yang and Lee remembered Feynman's words during one of their lunches in May. They decided to check physics journals and find out whether anyone had proved experimentally that the parity law held for weak interactions. They discovered that no one had.

The two young physicists now began designing experiments that could test the parity law in weak interactions. As Yang described it later, the basic idea of the experiments was this:

> One constructs two sets of experimental arrangements which are mirror images of each other, and which contain weak interactions. One then examines whether the two arrangements always give the same results in terms of the readings of their meters (or counters). If the results are not the same, one has an unequivocal proof that right-left symmetry . . . breaks down.

In late June, Lee and Yang published a paper in which they considered what would happen if the parity law did not always hold. They also described the experiments they had worked out. Their paper caused a great stir because most physicists could not see why a law that had been shown to be valid in most circumstances should fail in just a few.

A woman named Chien-shiung Wu, one of Lee's fellow physics professors at Columbia, was very interested in the two men's ideas. Like Lee and Yang, Wu came from China. She was older than they, having been born on May 29, 1912, in Liu Ho. Her father, the

Chien-shiung Wu, called "the reigning queen of nuclear physics," carried out the experiment that proved Lee and Yang's theory.   (American Institute of Physics, Emilio Segrè Visual Archives)

principal of a private school for girls, had encouraged his daughter to educate herself. She had decided while still in high school that she wanted to be a physicist.

Wu had studied at the National Central University in Nanking, from which she received a B.S. degree in 1936. She had then come to the United States to do graduate work. At the University of California's Berkeley campus she had studied under Ernest Lawrence, the inventor of the cyclotron. She had earned her Ph.D. in 1940. Two years later she had married a fellow Chinese-American student, Luke Chia-liu Yuan, with whom she later had a son, Vincent. She continued to use her maiden name after her marriage.

After teaching briefly at Smith College and Princeton, Wu had moved to Columbia in 1944. By then she was an expert on beta particles, high-energy electrons found in the atom's center or nucleus. The formation and breakdown of beta particles are weak interactions.

A superb experimentalist (it was said of her that "she has virtually never made a mistake in her experiments"), Wu was the perfect person to test Yang and Lee's theories. After she read their paper, she gave up a trip to Europe and Asia to begin one of the experiments they had suggested. It used a radioactive form of the element cobalt, cobalt-60, which gave off beta particles as its nuclei (plural of *nucleus*) broke down.

All atomic nuclei spin around an imaginary axis, just as the Earth does. Lee and Yang said that if a small piece of cobalt-60 could be exposed to a strong magnet, the magnetic field would make all the axes line up, just as iron filings line up when exposed to a magnet. If parity was conserved, half the nuclei would throw their beta particles out toward the north end of the magnetic field and half toward the south. If parity was not conserved, however, more particles would fly off in one direction than in the other. The difference could be measured by counters that detected beta particles.

The only problem was that at most temperatures, the cobalt-60 atoms would move so fast that the effect of the magnet would not be detectable. In order for the experiment to work, Wu would have to cool the cobalt to 0.01° above absolute zero, the temperature at which all atomic motion stops. (Absolute zero is about 460° below zero Fahrenheit.) Wu therefore went to the National Bureau of Standards

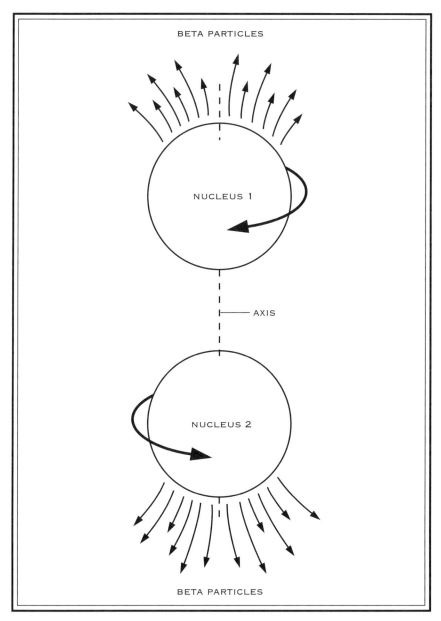

BETA PARTICLES

NUCLEUS 1

AXIS

NUCLEUS 2

BETA PARTICLES

Wu's experiment showed that radioactive cobalt nuclei gave off more beta particles in one direction than in the other as the nuclei broke down, or decayed. The direction in which most particles flew off depended on the direction in which a nucleus was spinning on its axis. The fact that the particles did not fly off equally in all directions showed that the law of conservation of parity did not hold for this type of subatomic action, called a weak interaction. (Dale Williams, based on a drawing by Katherine Macfarlane)

in Washington, D.C., the only place in the country with the complex machinery needed to cool material this much. There, with the help of bureau scientists, she performed the cobalt-60 experiment several times in December 1956. During this meticulous work she got an average of four hours' sleep a night. She said later that those hectic weeks were "like a nightmare. I wouldn't want to go through them again."

Yang and Lee probably did not sleep much better until Wu told them that her experiment had confirmed their theory. She found that most of the beta particles flew off in the direction opposite to that in which the cobalt-60 nuclei were spinning, showing that the nuclei behaved like left-handed screws. The fact that the nuclei had a preferred "handedness" proved that parity was not conserved in this weak interaction. A different experiment, performed by two other Columbia physicists a few days later, showed the same result.

Many physicists first heard details of these groundbreaking experiments at the annual meeting of the American Physical Society in late January 1957. The society's secretary later reported that for the session on the subject, a large hall was so packed that "some . . . members did everything but hang from the chandeliers." Indeed, until someone recognized him and let him through, Tsung Dao Lee could not even push his way into the hall.

The experiments shook physics because they proved that a basic rule that had been taken for granted was not true. That, in turn, brought many other assumptions into question. I. I. Rabi, winner of the 1944 Nobel Prize in physics, commented that because of Lee, Yang, and Wu's discovery, "a rather complete theoretical structure has been shattered at the base, and we are not sure how the pieces will be put together."

At the same time that disproving parity created doubt, it also created

I*t is the courage to doubt what has long been established, the incessant [constant] search for its verification and proof that pushed the wheel of science forward.*

—Chien-shiung Wu

hope that physicists, no longer held back by wrong information, could begin to learn what really happened inside atoms. Chien-shiung Wu said, "Physicists are now viewing Nature with a new understanding. . . . When we arrive at this understanding, we shall marvel how neatly all the elementary [subatomic] particles fit into the Great Scheme." Physicists hoped that their new understanding would eventually lead them to a "theory of everything" that would unite the four forces at work in the atom and explain how these forces constructed the universe.

The *New York Post* hailed the disproving of the law of parity as "the most important development in nuclear physics since the . . . unleashing of atomic energy." It brought prompt fame to Yang and Lee, which peaked when they won the Nobel Prize in physics in fall 1957—an amazingly short time after their discovery. Lee, not quite 31 years old, became the second-youngest Nobel winner ever. He and Yang were also the first Chinese to win the prize.

Wu was not included in the Nobel Prize, but she won several other important science awards, including the Research Corporation Award and Israel's Wolf Prize. In 1976 she won the National Medal of Science, the highest science award in the United States. Nobel Prize–winning physicist Emilio Segrè called her "the reigning queen of nuclear physics."

Yang, Lee, and Wu made no other discoveries that affected physics as much as their disproving of parity, but all had long and productive careers. Yang remained for some years at Princeton, where Lee again joined him in 1960. Lee returned to Columbia in 1964. Yang, meanwhile, became director of the Institute for Theoretical Physics at the State University of New York at Stony Brook in 1965.

Chien-shiung Wu became a full professor at Columbia the year after her parity experiment and remained there for the rest of her career. She performed other classic experiments, including one that had to be done in a salt mine 2,000 feet (3,200 km) below the Earth's surface. Another experiment examined the behavior of iron atoms in the blood of people with sickle-cell disease, an inherited blood disorder. Wu retired in 1981, and she died in 1997.

Chen Ning Yang and Tsung Dao Lee share Subrahmanyan Chandrasekhar's regard for simplicity, truth, and beauty in nature. Yang has said, "The . . . simplicity and . . . beauty of the symmetries that . . . evolve from complex experiments are, for the physicists, great sources of encouragement." Chien-shiung Wu's experiments show a similar feeling. Nobel Prize winner Polykarp Kusch said of her, "Professor Wu's experiments have . . . , by virtue of their elegance, a high esthetic quality." The work of all three scientists has helped to reveal both complexity and simplicity in the forces that shape the universe.

Chronology

MAY 29, 1912	Chien-shiung Wu born in Liu Ho, China
SEPTEMBER 22, 1922	Chen Ning Yang born in Hofei, China
NOVEMBER 24, 1926	Tsung Dao Lee born in Shanghai, China
1940	Wu receives Ph.D. from University of California
1944	Wu joins Columbia University
1944–1945	Lee and Yang come to University of Chicago
1948	Yang receives Ph.D. from University of Chicago
1950	Lee receives Ph.D. from University of Chicago
1953	Lee joins Columbia University
SPRING 1956	Richard Feynman suggests that law of parity conservation may not hold for weak interactions
JUNE 1956	Lee and Yang suggest ways to test parity law
DECEMBER 1956	Wu performs experiment that disproves parity law

FALL 1957	Lee and Yang win Nobel Prize in physics
1965	Yang joins State University of New York
1976	Wu wins National Medal of Science

Further Reading

Bernstein, Jeremy. "A Question of Parity." *The New Yorker*, May 12, 1962, pp. 50–104. Long, fascinating article provides background on Yang and Lee and describes their disproving of the law of conservation of parity.

"Death of a Law." *Time*, January 28, 1957, pp. 59–62. Describes the experiments that disproved the parity law and explains their importance.

"Lee, Tsung-Dao." *Current Biography 1958*. New York: H.W. Wilson, 1958. Concise biographical sketch of Lee, based on newspaper and magazine articles.

Noble, Iris. *Contemporary Women Scientists of America*. New York: Messner, 1979. For young adults. Contains a chapter on Chien-shiung Wu.

"Yang, Chen Ning." *Current Biography 1958*. New York: H.W. Wilson, 1958. Concise biographical sketch of Yang, based on newspaper and magazine articles.

Yount, Lisa. *Contemporary Women Scientists*. New York: Facts On File, 1994. For young adults. Contains a chapter on Chien-shiung Wu.

Har Gobind Khorana

(1922–)

What we look like, how healthy we are, even perhaps how we behave—all are determined to a great extent by genes, the units of biological information we inherit from our parents. Each cell in the human body contains about 100,000 genes, made of a complex chemical called DNA (deoxyribonucleic acid). These genes act like computer programs to specify each chemical the cell makes and each activity it performs.

Scientists truly began to understand genes only in the 1950s, after James Watson and Francis Crick worked out the structure of DNA. Crick and others determined that the arrangement of smaller molecules within each DNA molecule acted as a code to spell out instructions to the cell, much as the letters of an alphabet arranged in a certain order spell out words. An Indian-American scientist named Har Gobind Khorana played an important part in deciphering the DNA code and determining how it works in cells. Khorana also created the first artificial genes, an early milestone in the technology of genetic engineering.

Har Gobind Khorana helped to decipher the genetic code that carries the information that a living thing inherits from its parents. He also created the first artificial genes.
(photo Donna Coveney; MIT)

Har Gobind Khorana's family background was like Subrahmanyan Chandrasekhar's in some ways and different in others. Khorana's father, Ganpat Rai, worked for the British government in India, just as Chandrasekhar's did, but Khorana's lived in a tiny village rather than a city and was far from wealthy. The village, Raipur, was in a region called the Punjab, now a part of West Pakistan, and Khorana's father was its tax collector. He and his wife, Krishna Devi, had five children, of whom Har Gobind was the youngest. Khorana's birth date has been recorded as January 9, 1922, but he maintains that the true date is not known.

One thing Khorana's and Chandrasekhar's families shared was a strong belief in the value of education. Khorana's family was almost the only one in Raipur that could read and write. Har Gobind's schooling began under a large tree, where a teacher instructed the village boys. He then attended a nearby high school and went on to Punjab University in Lahore, the city where Subrahmanyan Chandrasekhar had been born. Majoring in chemistry, Khorana earned a B.S. in 1943 and a master's degree in 1945, both with honors.

Like Chandrasekhar, Khorana won a government scholarship to continue his studies in England. He went to the University of Liverpool, where he completed his Ph.D. work in 1948. By then he had decided to specialize in the chemistry of living things. He studied in Germany for a year, then did research at Cambridge University, where Chandrasekhar had done his graduate work. There Khorana became interested in nucleic acids: DNA and a related chemical called RNA (ribonucleic acid).

At that time, scientists had found evidence that nucleic acids carried inherited information, but they did not know the form in which the information existed or how cells used it. James Watson and Francis Crick, also working at Cambridge, began to change all that in 1953. They found that the huge DNA molecule is shaped like a twisted ladder, with each rung on the ladder being a pair of smaller molecules called bases. In DNA, there are four kinds of bases: adenine (A), cytosine (C), guanine (G), and thymine (T).

Adenine always pairs with thymine, and guanine always pairs with cytosine.

Crick and others proposed that the sequence of bases in DNA was a code that told a cell how to make vital chemicals called proteins. Proteins, like nucleic acids, contain small molecules put together in a certain order. The small molecules that make up proteins are called amino acids. The problem was that there are only four kinds of DNA bases, but there are 20 kinds of amino acids in humans.

Crick suggested that the nucleic acid code "word" representing each amino acid was made up of three bases in a certain order. There could be 64 (4 x 4 x 4) possible combinations of three bases, more than enough to specify 20 amino acids. But which combination stood for which amino acid?

In 1952, the year before Watson and Crick made their ground-breaking discovery, Har Gobind Khorana had moved to the University of British Columbia in Vancouver, Canada. He also married a Swiss woman, Esther Elizabeth Sibler. They later had three children, Julia, Emily, and Dave.

Khorana and his coworkers specialized in synthesizing certain kinds of complex compounds, or making them chemically from smaller units. These compounds came originally from the bodies of living things. Once the techniques were worked out, synthesizing them was usually cheaper than extracting them. Synthesis greatly increased the amount of these chemicals available for scientists to study.

Khorana moved to the University of Wisconsin in 1960. He then returned to his earlier interest in the nucleic acid code, which no one had yet deciphered.

By then, scientists knew that DNA makes proteins by first copying itself in the form of what is called messenger RNA (mRNA). RNA is like DNA except that a base named uracil (U) takes the place of the thymine in DNA. Messenger RNA then attracts molecules of another form of RNA, transfer RNA (tRNA). Each tRNA molecule contains just three bases—one of the three-letter "words" in the nucleic acid code. Like a tugboat towing a ship, it pulls along with it a molecule of the amino acid represented by its word. With the help of small bodies called ribosomes, tRNA molecules attach to the

PROTEIN SYNTHESIS

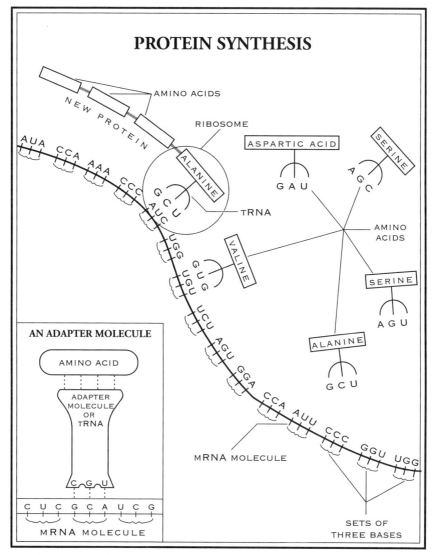

As a first step in making a protein, part of a DNA molecule (a gene) uses itself as a pattern to form a matching stretch of messenger RNA (mRNA). RNA is like DNA except that a base called uracil (U) substitutes for the thymine in DNA. In the messenger RNA, as in the DNA, each group of three bases is a "code word" representing one of the amino acids that can be combined to make a protein. When the messenger RNA moves into the cytoplasm (main body) of the cell, it attracts matching short stretches of transfer RNA (tRNA). Each molecule of transfer RNA acts like a tugboat, towing a single amino acid molecule. With the help of an organelle called a ribosome, the transfer RNA molecules lock onto the matching parts of the messenger RNA. The amino acids they carry are then joined, forming a protein. Har Gobind Khorana and other scientists used this process of protein formation to help them decipher the genetic code.   (Facts On File)

mRNA in a sequence dictated by the order of the bases in the mRNA. The amino acid molecules carried by the tRNA also line up, and another chemical links them together to form a protein.

Marshall Nirenberg of the National Institutes of Health (NIH), a group of large government-sponsored medical research institutes in Bethesda, Maryland, deciphered the first word in the nucleic acid code in 1964. He synthesized mRNA containing only uracil and put it in a test tube along with ribosomes, tRNA, and all 20 amino acids. He showed that the mixture produced a protein made entirely of the amino acid phenylalanine. This meant that U-U-U in RNA (T-T-T in DNA) had to be the code word for phenylalanine.

Now the race to crack the rest of the code was on, and Har Gobind Khorana became a leader in that race. He synthesized all 64 three-base combinations of RNA and DNA and used these pure compounds to verify the meaning of each "word" of the code. He also showed that some amino acids were represented by more than one sequence of three bases and that some three-base groups signaled the start or end of a protein molecule.

By 1966, the laboratories of Khorana, Nirenberg, and Robert W. Holley of Cornell University had completely deciphered the genetic code. These three men shared the Nobel Prize in physiology or medicine for their work in 1968. Khorana and Nirenberg also were awarded the Albert and Mary Lasker Award, the country's highest award for medical research, and Columbia University's Louisa Gross Horwitz Prize in that year.

The work that earns a scientist the Nobel Prize normally is the peak of that person's achievement. Khorana, however, went on to even greater things. On June 2, 1970, he announced that he and his coworkers had synthesized the first artificial gene. The gene, which contained the code for making the tRNA molecule that captured phenylalanine in yeast, was just 77 base pairs long. Most human genes, by contrast, contain millions of base pairs.

At the same time he announced the creation of the artificial gene, Khorana said that he was moving to the Massachusetts Institute of Technology (MIT). "You stay intellectually alive longer if you change your environment every so often," he noted. He has remained at MIT ever since.

Khorana announced in 1973 that he had made a second artificial gene, 126 base pairs long, that coded for a different kind of tRNA. The natural gene it duplicated came from a common intestinal bacterium called *Escherichia coli*, which was often used for experiments in genetics.

Khorana had been unable to show that his artificial genes could actually make tRNA because they lacked the groups of bases that provided the start

*S*urvival of our civilization is not . . . going to be possible without proper use of science.

—Har Gobind Khorana

and stop signals for chemical production. He spent the next several years figuring out the base sequence for these parts of the *E. coli* gene.

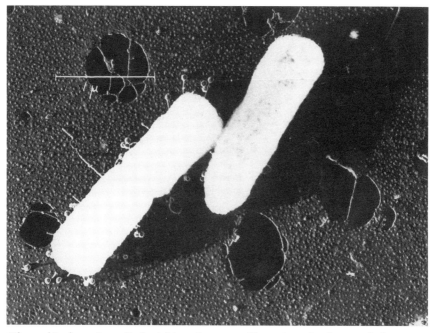

These white bacteria are Escherichia coli, *a type of bacterium that lives in the human intestine. The dark particles next to them are a type of virus called lambda, which infects these bacteria. Khorana inserted his artificial* E. coli *transfer RNA gene into lambda, which in turn put it into the genome of a type of* E. coli *that could not make that kind of tRNA. The bacteria then became able to make the tRNA, showing that Khorana's gene worked.* (American Society for Microbiology Archives Collection)

HAR GOBIND KHORANA

In 1976 he said that he had finally made a complete artificial form of the gene.

Khorana first showed that his gene could make its tRNA when combined with suitable "building block" chemicals in a test tube. He then used early genetic engineering techniques to place his artificial gene into the genome, or collection of genes, of a virus that infected *E. coli*. He knew of a type of *E. coli* that lacked the natural form of the gene he had made. When the altered virus infected these bacteria, it inserted the artificial gene into their genome along with its own genes. The bacteria then became able to make the tRNA. This proved that Khorana's gene really worked.

Har Gobind Khorana's cracking of the genetic code and development of methods for synthesizing genes laid part of the groundwork for the technology of genetic engineering, in which scientists change genes or transfer them from one living thing to another for human benefit. Khorana believed that chemical synthesis would be the best way to understand and alter genes. In fact, synthesis has proved impractical for most genes because the genes are so large and complex. Khorana's work nonetheless played an important part in the discovery of the basic nature of genes and how they function.

Chronology

JANUARY 9, 1922	Har Gobind Khorana born in Raipur, India
1948	obtains Ph.D. from University of Liverpool

1948–1952	studies in Germany and England
1952	James Watson and Francis Crick work out structure of DNA; Khorana moves to University of British Columbia in Vancouver, Canada
1960	moves to University of Wisconsin
1964	Marshall Nirenberg deciphers first "word" of DNA code
1964–1966	Khorana synthesizes all 64 DNA code "words" and helps to learn their meaning
1968	wins Lasker Award and Nobel Prize
JUNE 2, 1970	synthesizes first artificial gene; moves to MIT
1973	synthesizes *E. coli* gene
1976	synthesizes gene with start and stop signals; shows that it works in test tubes and bacteria

Further Reading

"A Gene at Last." *Science News*, June 6, 1970, p. 547. Describes Khorana's synthesis of first artificial gene.

"A 126-Unit Artificial Gene." *Science News*, September 1, 1973, p. 132. Describes Khorana's synthesis of the main part of an *E. coli* gene.

"Khorana, Har Gobind." *Current Biography 1970.* New York: H.W. Wilson, 1970. Main source of biographical information on Khorana.

Singer, Maxine F. "1968 Nobel Laureate in Medicine or Physiology." *Science*, October 25, 1968, pp. 433–436. Describes the Nobel-winning work of Khorana, Marshall Nirenberg, and Robert Holley in deciphering the genetic code. Difficult reading.

Samuel C. C. Ting discovered a new type of subatomic particle. He has also studied the mysterious material called antimatter, which completely destroys any matter that it touches. (photo Donna Coveney; MIT)

Samuel Chao Chung Ting

(1936–)

Imagine that you have a twin who is exactly like you in some ways but opposite in others. Your faces are alike, for instance, but one of you has light hair and the other dark. Sometimes you go around together, but at other times you feel like murdering each other.

In the world of subatomic particles, such strange twins actually exist. Each kind of particle that makes up matter has an antiparticle with an opposite electrical charge or direction of motion. Sometimes a pair of these opposites is bound together to make a third particle. If quantities of matter and antimatter come too close, however, the result is what physicist and science writer James Trefil calls "the most powerful explosion known in nature." It destroys both substances, turning them into pure energy.

Tsung Dao Lee and Chen Ning Yang investigated one kind of subatomic twins, particles that differed in parity. Another Chinese-American physicist, Samuel C. C. Ting, studies the pairs of twin particles that make up matter and antimatter. In doing so, he has discovered a new kind of subatomic particle and changed physicists' understanding of the atom. He now leads a hunt for antimatter in outer space.

☆ ☆ ☆

Samuel Chao Chung Ting was born in Ann Arbor, Michigan, on January 27, 1936. At the time, both his parents were visiting professors at the University of Michigan. His father, Kuan Hai Ting, taught engineering; his mother, Jeanne M. Wong Ting, was a psychology professor. They returned to China, their homeland, when Sam was three months old.

China was at war during much of Sam's childhood, and his family sometimes had to flee the fighting. Between the war and their university duties, his parents had little time for him. His schooling was mostly what he taught himself. When Sam was 12, however, Communists took control of mainland China, and his family moved to the nearby large island of Taiwan. There he had to join a strict, formal school system. The change was abrupt, but he did so well that he was put in the best class of the finest high school in Taipei, the island's capital.

When Sam was ready for college, he returned to the University of Michigan. He graduated with bachelor's degrees in mathematics and physics in 1959. A year later he earned his master's degree there, and in 1962 he became a Ph.D. in physics. He still loves to watch Michigan football games.

Like Chen Ning Yang, Tsung Dao Lee, and Chien-shiung Wu, Samuel Ting was fascinated by the subatomic world. After earning his doctorate, he worked for a year at the European Organization for Nuclear Research in Geneva, Switzerland, known as CERN for the initials of its French name. He then moved to Columbia University in 1964. In 1969 he went to the Massachusetts Institute of Technology (MIT), with which he has remained connected ever since, though he has continued to work in Europe part time as well. In addition to CERN he has worked at DESY, a large nuclear physics center in Hamburg, Germany.

Ting's personal life changed during these years as well. During the 1960s he and his first wife had two daughters, Jeanne and Amy. In

1985 he married Susan Marks, a fellow scientist. They have one son, Christopher.

Some of Ting's work in Germany involved electrons (negatively charged subatomic particles) and their "twin" antimatter particles, called positrons because they have a positive charge. In 1971 he began a new set of experiments on electrons and positrons at Brookhaven National Laboratory on Long Island, New York. He used Brookhaven's Alternating Gradient Synchrotron (AGS), in which protons traveling at almost the speed of light smashed against a target made of the metallic element beryllium. The protons disintegrated into a hail of particles, including electrons, positrons, and perhaps other particles never detected before. James Trefil describes such "atom smasher" experiments as being "like trying to learn about architecture by bombarding buildings with artillery shells and looking at the flying bricks coming from the explosion."

Ting decided to look for new particles with a mass of between 3 and 4 billion electron volts, three to four times as heavy as a proton. (Physicists describe the mass of subatomic particles as the amount of energy into which the particles can be converted.) Modifying a design he had created at DESY, he invented a detector sensitive enough to pick out one such particle from the results of between a million and 100 million collisions. Currently accepted theory said that few, if any, particles should exist in this mass range, but that did not discourage Ting. As he said later, "I am happy to eat . . . dinners with theorists, but to spend your life doing what they tell you is a waste of time." Like Chien-shiung Wu, Ting has been called a "consummate experimentalist," but he would rather design his own experiments than carry out those suggested by others.

In August 1974, Ting's group confirmed his seemingly wild guess. His detector showed evidence of 100 times more particles with a mass of just over 3 billion electron volts than theory predicted. It seemed likely that he was seeing a new kind of particle. The mystery particles, which had no electric charge, had a lifetime 1,000 times longer than expected. Even so, they existed for just one hundred millionth of a trillionth of a second, such a brief time that Ting's detector could not count the particles themselves but only their decay products.

Ting discovered the J particle in experiments that used the Alternating Gradient Synchrotron (AGS), an atom-smasher belonging to Brookhaven National Laboratory on Long Island, New York. Here two technicians do routine maintenance on the AGS while a third uses a bicycle to shorten his journey around the synchrotron's half-mile ring. During repeated journeys around this circular "race track," subatomic particles are accelerated until they reach almost the speed of light. They then smash into a target, shattering into energy and a rain of new particles. (Brookhaven National Laboratory)

After repeating and checking his work for two months, Ting finally felt sure that his group had indeed found a new particle. He decided to call it the J particle. He later said he chose this letter because it is the symbol for a quality called rotational momentum, of which the particle had a large amount. Other physicists have pointed out, however, that the letter *J* is similar in shape to the Chinese character *Ting*—so Ting, perhaps unconsciously, was also naming the particle after himself.

At the same time, across the country and unknown to Ting, a different group of physicists, headed by Burton Richter, was equally hard at work at the Stanford Linear Accelerator (SLAC) in the hills of Palo Alto, California. They were exploring the same reaction Ting's group was, but from the opposite end. They wanted to see what was produced when electrons and positrons collided and destroyed each other, creating energy that was transformed into new particles. On the weekend of November 9 and 10, Richter's group discovered a particle with the same mass as the one Ting had found. They named it after the Greek letter *psi* because the track it made in the group's detectors looked something like that letter.

By coincidence, Ting visited SLAC on Monday, November 11. He and Richter met in a corridor during a break from the committee meeting they were both attending. "Burt, I have some interesting physics to tell you about," Ting told Richter. "Sam, I have some interesting physics to tell *you* about," Richter replied. When the two men described their experiments to each other, it became obvious that they had discovered the same particle.

Like Lee, Yang, and Wu's disproving of the parity law, Ting and Richter's discovery of the J/psi particle caused a sensation because it changed physicists' understanding of the atom. Physicists had come to believe that subatomic particles were actually combinations of theoretical particles called quarks. They had found evidence for the existence of three kinds of quarks, which they called up, down, and strange. Theory had predicted a fourth type of quark, possessing a quality that had been dubbed charm. (Faced with qualities that have no equivalent in the ordinary world, physicists apparently just choose names that appeal to them.) No physical evidence for charm quarks had been found, however.

SAMUEL CHAO CHUNG TING

39

Burton Richter, head of a group of physicists working at the Stanford Linear Accelerator in Palo Alto, California, discovered the new particle at almost the same time Samuel Ting did. Richter's group named the particle after the Greek letter psi.   (photo Chuck Painter, Stanford University News Service)

Certain features of the J/psi particle suggested that it was made up of a charm quark and its opposite, an antiquark that also possessed charm. The two circle each other until they collide, resulting in mutual destruction. Richter and others soon showed that J/psi was the first of a whole new family of particles made of charm quarks.

Proving the existence of charm, according to *Science News* magazine, "required fundamental revisions in the whole theory of subatomic particles." As had happened with Yang and Lee, Ting and Richter's discovery was so important that it won them a Nobel Prize soon after it was completed. The two men shared the prize for physics in 1976.

Samuel Ting has won many awards in addition to the Nobel Prize. They include the Ernest Orlando Lawrence Award from the U.S. Department of Energy (1976), the Eringen Medal from the Society of English Scientists (1977), the DeGasperi Award in Science from the government of Italy (1988), and the Golden Leopard Award for Excellence and the Gold Medal of Science (1988).

Ting has been associated with "big science" for most of his career. In the 1980s and early 1990s, for instance, he headed CERN's L3 project, which cost $350 million and employed some 600 physicists. Its chief piece of equipment was the Large Electron-Positron Collider (LEP), a tunnel 17 miles around that is a sort of race track for particles. After being boosted to nearly the speed of light, the particles collide inside a complex detector system in an electromagnet. The magnet, in turn, is housed in a four-story octagonal building 100 feet below ground. On first seeing the building in 1989, Ting commented, "This is crazy. . . . It can't be this size."

In 1993, however, Ting turned from big science to small. Working mostly with two other scientists, Michael

T*he collaboration Ting leads is a bit like an army—during group meetings he slowly paces the aisles, dressed in a dark suit, hands clasped behind his back, like a general reviewing his troops.*

—Robert Crease,
Science magazine

Salamon and Steve Ahlen, he is now exploring a different aspect of the search that led him to the J particle.

Theorists believe that at its birth in the gigantic explosion called the Big Bang, the universe consisted of equal amounts of matter and antimatter. No trace of antimatter above the subatomic level has been found in nature, however. It seems clear that our galaxy and all nearby ones are made up solely of matter. But what about the rest of the universe? Could there somewhere be antigalaxies, filled with anti-stars? And if there are, can they ever be detected?

Ting, Salamon, and Ahlen think they can. The Earth is constantly bombarded by high-energy particles from space called cosmic rays. Some of these rays come from outside our galaxy, and a few may even come from more than 100 million light-years away, the distance up to which scientists are sure that the universe contains no antimatter. A cosmic ray made of antimatter should leave certain signs in the right kind of detector. Finding such rays would show that galaxies made of antimatter exist somewhere in the universe.

Detectors in high-altitude balloons have found no antimatter rays, but this may not mean that such rays don't exist. Only one in every 100,000, perhaps even one in a million, cosmic rays is thought to come from outside the Milky Way. No experiment done so far has looked at enough rays to rule out rays made of antimatter. A better detector, placed above the Earth's interfering atmosphere, might be able to settle the question.

Ting and the others have designed a new type of antimatter detector based on the ones Ting invented for his earlier projects. It can examine billions of cosmic rays. It uses a small, powerful magnet to bend the paths of electrically charged particles that pass near it. Because matter and antimatter particles of the same type have opposite charges, their paths should bend in opposite directions.

The three men named their device the Antimatter Spectrometer, or AMS. They have persuaded NASA to attach it to the proposed international space station *Alpha* for three years beginning in 2001. "For a very small amount of money we have the potential for blockbuster science," says Dan Goldin, head of NASA.

What the AMS finds out could revolutionize astronomers' under-standing of the universe, just as Ting's earlier work did for the atom.

It could give some indication of whether half the universe really is made of antimatter. If the antimatter is not there, the experiment may provide ideas about when, how, and why it disappeared.

Furthermore, astronomers have found evidence that the universe contains much more mass than can be accounted for by all the known stars and galaxies that give off light. No one knows what this "dark" matter is—yet it apparently makes up more than 80 percent of the universe. One possibility is that at least some of it either is antimatter or decays into certain kinds of antiparticles. Ting's detector may give some idea of whether this is so.

Sam Ting hopes that the AMS will be the "one more interesting experiment" he has a chance to do before he retires. It is part of his lifetime task, which has been, he says, "exploring the unknown."

The great thing about Ting is that he is guided by general principles. Is there a compelling argument why there is no antimatter? No. Has anyone looked for antimatter at the sensitivity you need to? No. Then you look for antimatter. It's as simple as that.

—Steve Ahlen

Chronology

JANUARY 27, 1936	Samuel Chao Chung Ting born in Ann Arbor, Michigan
1962	obtains Ph.D. from University of Michigan
1964	joins faculty of Columbia University
1969	moves to MIT
1971	begins work at Brookhaven National Laboratory

FALL 1974	discovers J particle
FALL 1976	awarded Nobel Prize in physics
1980S–EARLY 1990S	heads L3 project at CERN
1993	begins search for antimatter cosmic rays

Further Reading

Bjorken, J. D. "The 1976 Nobel Prize in Physics." *Science*, November 19, 1976, pp. 825–826, 865–866. Account of discovery of the J/psi particle, which won the prize for Samuel Ting and Burton Richter. Difficult reading.

Mann, Charles C. "Army of Physicists Struggle to Discover Proof of a Scot's Brainchild." *Smithsonian*, March 1989, pp. 107–114. Describes CERN's L3 project, which Ting headed.

Metz, William D. "Two New Particles Found: Physicists Baffled and Delighted." *Science*, December 4, 1974, pp. 909–911. Describes discovery of J/psi particle soon after it was announced. Difficult reading.

Morey, Janet Nomura, and Wendy Dunn. *Famous Asian Americans.* New York: Cobblehill Books, 1992. For young adults. Includes a good chapter on Ting, focusing on his discovery of the J particle and the L3 project.

Taubes, Gary. "The Antimatter Mission." *Discover*, April 1996, pp. 73–79. Describes Ting's collaboration with Michael Salamon and Steve Ahlen to search for antimatter cosmic rays in space.

Trefil, James S. "New Particles Jolt Established Theories of Ultimate Matter." *Smithsonian*, July 1975, pp. 96–102. Enjoyable account of the discovery of the J/psi particle, explaining its importance.

Susumu Tonegawa

(1939–)

The possibility is the stuff of nightmares or blockbuster science fiction movies: A microorganism from, say, Mars reaches Earth, riding in a meteorite or a returning spaceship. No living thing on our planet has ever encountered this microbe. If it causes disease, everything will be defenseless against it—right?

Wrong. The human immune system, the mixture of blood cells and chemicals that protects the body against invasion, is so flexible that it could mount a defense against even a challenge like this. Potentially it can attack billions of different enemies.

Until the 1970s, no one understood how the immune system could be so versatile. Susumu Tonegawa, a Japanese-American molecular biologist, helped to unravel that mystery. In doing so, he not only greatly increased the understanding of the immune system but also changed scientists' knowledge of how genes work.

☆ ☆ ☆

Susumu Tonegawa discovered how the immune system can defend the body against billions of different enemies.   (photo Bachrach; MIT)

Susumu Tonegawa was born in Nagoya, Japan, on September 5, 1939. His father, a businessman, still lives in Japan. Tonegawa went to college at Kyoto University, from which he graduated in 1963. He then continued his studies at the University of California at San Diego. He earned his Ph.D. in 1968. He specialized in molecular biology, the study of the structure and function of the chemicals in living things. In 1971 he moved to the Basel Institute for Immunology in Switzerland. He remained there for a decade, during which he did some of his most important work.

By the 1960s, scientists knew that the immune system can defend itself against disease-causing microbes or other foreign substances in several ways. One of the most important involves white blood cells called B cells. (Red cells, the most common kind of cells in the blood, carry oxygen through the body. The larger, less common white cells are part of the immune system.) These B cells make chemicals named antibodies, which fit into other chemicals on the surface of foreign particles as a key fits into a lock. Once attached, the antibody sends an alarm signal, attracting other kinds of white cells that attack and destroy the invader.

B cells can make huge numbers of different kinds of antibodies, each able to attach itself to a different foreign chemical, but no one knew exactly how they managed. Some biologists thought that instructions for all the antibodies were somehow contained in the germ line, the genes that an individual inherits from his or her parents. This seemed unlikely, however, because a human has only about 100,000 genes, and these must provide instructions for many proteins besides antibodies. Just a handful of genes was likely to carry antibody instructions.

A second theory said that the power to make so many different antibodies emerged after birth through changes, or mutations, in the genes of individual cells. Yet this, too, seemed unlikely because as far as scientists knew, information in genes seldom changed during an organism's development.

In 1965 William Dreyer of Caltech and J. C. Bennett of the University of Alabama School of Medicine suggested a possible answer to this puzzle. They pointed out that an antibody molecule, which is shaped something like two overlapping copies of the letter

Y, is made up of several parts. Two smaller molecules called heavy chains form the inner arms and the double stem of the Y. Attached to each heavy chain arm, seemingly doubling it, is another molecule called a light chain. The two light chains of each antibody are alike, and so are the two heavy chains.

There are several types of antibodies, and the main part of the molecule is the same in all antibodies of each type. Because it seldom changes, this part of the molecule has been named the constant region (abbreviated by the letter *C*). The area around the tips of the Y's arms, however, differs greatly from antibody to antibody. It is therefore called the variable region (V). Both light chains and heavy chains have constant and variable regions. The variable regions of the light and heavy chains together form the part of the antibody that attaches to foreign chemicals.

Dreyer and Bennett suggested that, even though each chain in an antibody is a single molecule, the code for making it might be

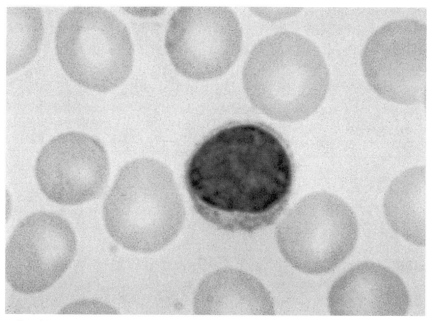

White blood cells like the large, dark cell in the center of this photograph help to defend the body against disease-causing microbes. Some kinds of white cells make the antibodies that Susumu Tonegawa studied. The lighter cells in the picture are red blood cells, which carry oxygen. (American Society of Hematology Slide Bank)

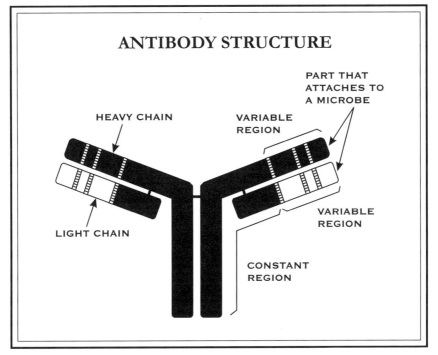

ANTIBODY STRUCTURE

PART THAT
ATTACHES TO
A MICROBE

HEAVY CHAIN

VARIABLE
REGION

VARIABLE
REGION

LIGHT CHAIN

CONSTANT
REGION

An antibody molecule is shaped like a double letter Y. The inner arms and double stem of the Y are formed from smaller molecules called heavy chains. Another small molecule called a light chain is attached to each arm of the Y. Each light chain and each heavy chain have a variable and a constant region. The constant region is the same in all antibodies of a certain type, but the variable regions differ from antibody to antibody. The variable regions attach to the surfaces of microbes and other foreign substances, marking them for destruction. (Katherine Macfarlane)

contained in two separate stretches of DNA. One stretch might specify the constant region for all antibodies of a certain type. The variable region's code might be contained in any one of a number of other DNA pieces.

The problem with Dreyer and Bennett's theory was that it required two things that were not then known to exist. One was split genes (separated stretches of DNA that coded for a single molecule). The other was a mechanism that would allow genes or gene parts to move during a living thing's lifetime. Such a mechanism would be needed to bring the stretches of DNA together so they could make a single protein molecule.

Three different laboratories, including Susumu Tonegawa's, set out to test this theory in the early 1970s, the same period during which Har Gobind Khorana was making artificial genes. Tonegawa and his chief coworker, Nobumichi Hozumi, reported in 1976 that, just as Dreyer and Bennett had predicted, the codes for the variable and constant regions in an antibody light chain were on different stretches of DNA.

Tonegawa reasoned that if the Dreyer-Bennett theory was right, the gene arrangement in the immature B cells of mouse embryos (mice at an early stage of development before birth) should be different from that in mature B cells. Sure enough, he and Hozumi found that the DNA stretches that coded for the variable and constant regions of the light chain were far apart in mouse embryo cells. In mature B cells, however, the two were close together. During development, pieces of DNA had somehow moved.

Tonegawa's experiments showed that the body can do its own genetic engineering. In 1985 he wrote in *Scientific American,* "Antibody genes offer dramatic evidence that DNA is not an inert archive but can be altered during the life span of an individual." He has compared this gene shuffling to moving boxcars from one part of a freight train to another.

Tonegawa and two scientists from Harvard next worked out the base sequence of the DNA that coded for an antibody light chain in adult mouse B cells. To their surprise, they found that, although the DNA segment that coded for the chain's variable region and the segment that coded for the constant region were close together in these cells, the two were not right next to each other. They were separated by another stretch of DNA some 1,250 base pairs long that did not seem to code for anything. Such "blank" stretches, called introns, were later found in most

> I *still remember the day I went to the lab and saw the results. I was very glad to see the experiment worked. But it took . . . months to realize what the impact of this was.*
>
> —Susumu Tonegawa

ASIAN-AMERICAN SCIENTISTS

50

genes of higher organisms. This was one of the first introns discovered in the cells of a mammal.

Tonegawa and his fellow scientists got another surprise when they worked out the base sequence that coded for the variable region of an antibody light chain in embryo mice and then used this sequence to form a protein. Their protein was about 13 amino acids shorter than the natural one. Another molecular biologist, Philip Leder, got similar results with a different light-chain variable region segment. He and Tonegawa agreed that the code for the missing piece of the chain must be contained in a separate, undiscovered gene fragment.

Christine Brack, a researcher in Tonegawa's laboratory, found the missing piece of the puzzle. The group named it J, for "joining." J is thousands of base pairs away from the rest of the variable region gene segment in embryo mice. As antibody-producing cells mature, however, the two segments become linked. They are separated from the constant region gene segment by the intron.

Leroy Hood, a researcher at Caltech who was also studying antibody genes, found that the heavy chain gene, too, was made of several separate parts—four, to be exact. In addition to the V, C, and J segments, Hood and his coworkers discovered a segment that they called D, for diversity. It lay between the V and J segments.

Just as the same letters of the alphabet can be arranged in different order to form different words—*seal* and *sale*, for instance—the proteins made by these gene segments can be combined in many ways to form different antibody molecules. For the heavy chain alone, humans have about 150 possible forms of the V segment, 12 forms of the D segment, and 6 forms of the J segment. These can make almost 11,000 possible combinations ($150 \times 12 \times 6$). Combining a similar number of variants of light chain V and J regions makes about 1,000 different light chain types. Since any light chain can combine with any heavy chain, the number of possible combinations goes up to 11 million. Finally, just as the old body-cell mutation theory had predicted, spontaneous changes occur in antibody genes much more easily than in most genes. These mutations create still more antibody variations.

All these factors show how billions of different antibodies can be created by just a few genes. As Tonegawa has explained:

It's like when GM [General Motors] builds a car they want to meet the specific needs of many customers. If they custom-make each car, it is not economical, so they make different parts, then they assemble it in different ways, and therefore one can make different cars. It's a matter of how you assemble those pieces.

In 1981 Susumu Tonegawa returned to the United States and joined the faculty of the Massachusetts Institute of Technology (MIT). Like Har Gobind Khorana and Samuel Ting, he has remained there ever since. Tonegawa works at the university's Center for Cancer Research.

At MIT, Tonegawa studied T cells, another kind of white cell in the immune system. Some T cells have molecules on their surfaces that, like the antibodies made by B cells, attach to molecules on the surface of foreign substances. Unlike antibodies, however, these T cell molecules stick to surfaces that contain a combination of foreign and familiar molecules (ones that normally appear on body cells).

Tonegawa thinks T cells may help the body fight off virus infections. Viruses penetrate body cells and reproduce inside them. Infected cells have both virus proteins and their own proteins on their surfaces. When a T cell recognizes this combination of proteins on a cell, it marks that cell for destruction. The cell is then removed before the viruses inside it can finish reproducing and spread through the body.

*[*S*usumu] doesn't have any prejudices before he begins work. He has a pure mind before nature and science.*

—Mayumi Tonegawa
wife of Susumu Tonegawa

In 1987 Tonegawa's continuing work on the immune system won him the Lasker Award and then, a month later, the Nobel Prize in physiology or medicine. Tonegawa shared the Lasker Award with Philip Leder and Leroy Hood, but his Nobel Prize was not shared.

Tonegawa's fellow scientists were not surprised that he had won the awards. For instance, David Baltimore, director of the Whitehead Institute, said, "The immune system is the key defense the body has against infectious disease, [and] Susumu's work provided the key to how that system functions. It can't be overestimated how important that . . . was."

In recent years, Tonegawa's research has turned in a different direction. He still studies genes and body chemicals, but he is now looking at chemicals that affect the way a living thing behaves. He has found, for instance, that mice that lack a gene for a chemical that changes the activity of an important substance in nerves are much more aggressive than other mice. They also do not act fearful when faced with an experience that would frighten normal mice, such as a mild electric shock. It is possible that some criminals or other people who engage in risky and aggressive behavior may also lack this gene or a related one.

Susumu Tonegawa's work has laid the foundation for solving many riddles about the immune system. Scientists can draw on it, for instance, to learn how and why the body rejects transplanted organs and, perhaps, to prevent this rejection. They can use it to learn why the immune system sometimes attacks the body's own cells, causing disease. It has also provided new information about how genes function and change. It is a classic example of groundbreaking basic science.

Chronology

SEPTEMBER 5, 1939	Susumu Tonegawa born in Nagoya, Japan
1965	Dreyer and Bennett suggest that two or more DNA segments may contain code for antibody molecule
1968	Tonegawa earns Ph.D. from University of California at San Diego
1971	moves to Basel Institute for Immunology
1976	proves Dreyer and Bennett's theory

LATE 1970s	shows that gene segments can move as cells develop; shows that light chain genes contain several parts
1981	joins faculty of MIT
EARLY 1980s	does research on T cells
FALL 1987	wins Lasker Award and Nobel Prize in medicine
1990s	investigates chemicals that affect behavior

Further Reading

Davis, Joel. *Defending the Body.* New York: Atheneum, 1989. Describes research on the immune system, including Tonegawa's work.

Leder, Philip. "The Genetics of Antibody Diversity," in William E. Paul, ed., *Immunology: Recognition and Response.* New York: W. H. Freeman, 1991. Describes what Tonegawa, Leder, and Hood learned about antibody diversity. Difficult reading.

Marx, Jean L. "Antibody Research Garners Nobel Prize." *Science,* October 23, 1987, pp. 484–485. Describes research on antibody diversity that won Tonegawa the Nobel Prize.

Paul Ching-wu Chu

(1941–)

In 1987, news articles predicted that a new technology was going to change the world. It would let people ride on trains that sped along at 300 mph (480 kmh), lifted above the ground by magnets. It would make computers 50 times more powerful than existing ones and electric power almost free.

A decade later, reality has set in, and predictions are less spectacular. Still, they are exciting enough. This same new technology, experts now say, is likely to increase the capacity of cellular telephone base stations by as much as 10 times. It will allow doctors to explore the heart and brain with a sensitivity never possible before. It may not make electricity free, but it can reduce rates by making power transmission and storage more efficient.

This technology is based on superconductivity, the power to transmit an electric current without waste. Whatever it achieves will owe much to the work of a Chinese-born scientist, Paul Ching-wu Chu. Chu has played a key role in changing superconductivity from an obscure laboratory phenomenon into a tool with immense power.

Paul Chu discovered substances that became superconducting, or able to conduct electricity without loss to resistance, at higher temperatures than any known before. Such substances potentially could revolutionize electric power transmission and storage, transportation, computers, and other technology. (University of Houston Media Services)

ASIAN-AMERICAN SCIENTISTS

☆ ☆ ☆

Ching-wu Chu was born in Hunan, China, on December 2, 1941, but he grew up on the nearby island of Taiwan. Even as a high school student he was a tinkerer. His favorite hobby was taking apart old radios and putting them back together.

Ching-wu first went to college at Cheng-Kung University, from which he earned a B.S. degree in 1962. He then moved to the United States and began calling himself by his baptismal name, Paul. He took his master's degree from Fordham University in New York City in 1965 and earned his Ph.D. in physics from the University of California at San Diego in 1968.

A teacher of Chu's at San Diego, Bernd Matthias, was one of the few physicists interested in a then obscure phenomenon called super-conductivity. Discovered by Dutch physicist Heike Onnes in 1911, superconductivity lets materials conduct electricity without loss from resistance.

Electricity is, basically, a flow of electrons (negatively charged subatomic particles). Materials that allow electrons to flow through them fairly easily, such as metals, are called conductors. Even in conductors, a certain number of electrons collide with other electrons in the atoms of the material and bounce out of the flowing stream. This process, resistance, wastes 10 to 20 percent of the electrical energy in a current by turning it into heat. In superconducting materials, however, electrons travel in pairs instead of singly. This somehow protects them from collisions and reduces resistance to zero.

Superconducting materials theoretically could save a tremendous amount of energy and money. Unfortunately, as far as anyone knew, superconductivity could be achieved only within a few degrees of absolute zero. Absolute zero is zero degrees on the Kelvin scale, the temperature scale physicists use, or $-460°$ Fahrenheit. By the 1970s, the highest temperature at which superconductivity had been seen was $23°$ K.

As Chien-shiung Wu discovered during her experiment to test the law of parity conservation, cooling any material to below about $-400°$ F is difficult. It requires liquid helium, which is costly and hard to

PAUL CHING-WU CHU

57

handle. Only a few uses of superconducting materials, such as in the powerful magnets in the atom smashers with which Samuel Ting

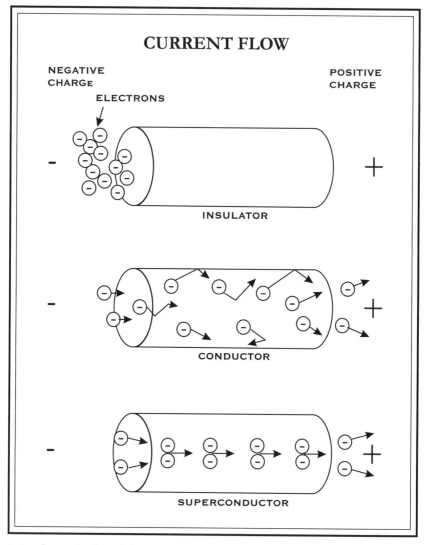

CURRENT FLOW

In insulators, the flow of electrons (electric current) is blocked almost completely by resistance because electrons in the materials are tightly bound to atoms and thus cannot move. Electrons in conductors are bound more loosely and therefore have more freedom to move, but some are still deflected by resistance, and their energy is lost as heat. In superconductors, by contrast, no electrical energy is lost to resistance. Electrons in a super- conductor travel in pairs that move in step with each other, which protects them against being deflected. (Katherine Macfarlane)

worked, were important enough to justify such expense. Most physicists doubted that this situation would ever change. Bernd Matthias was one of the few exceptions. His student, Paul Chu, became another.

Two other physicists who believed that superconductivity might someday become practical worked in Zurich, Switzerland. Their names were Karl Alex Müller and Georg Bednorz. Their jobs at a research facility owned by International Business Machines (IBM) had nothing to do with superconductivity, but they researched it as a hobby.

Instead of looking for superconductors among metals and metal alloys, as most researchers had, Müller decided in 1983 to examine the family of hard, brittle metal oxides (compounds containing metals and oxygen) called ceramics. Pottery bowls and china plates are everyday examples of ceramics. Ceramics seemed unlikely candidates for superconductors because, at ordinary temperatures, they conducted electricity so poorly that they were used as insulators to stop a current's flow. Nonetheless, after many tries, Müller and Bednorz found on January 27, 1986, that ceramics made by combining oxygen with a mixture of the elements lanthanum, barium, and copper did indeed become superconducting at much higher temperatures than any other materials tested so far. To be sure, the temperature required was still a chilly –397° F, but it was a definite improvement, the first in decades.

Müller and Bednorz kept their work quiet at first. "We didn't tell anybody what we were doing because we would have had difficulty convincing our more knowledgeable colleagues that what we were doing wasn't crazy," Bednorz said later. When they did publish an account of their research, they chose a small German physics journal. Few physicists paid their article any attention.

Again, however, there were exceptions, and Paul Chu was one of them. By this time he was at the University of Houston in Texas, having transferred there in 1979 after almost a decade at Cleveland State University in Ohio. Chu worked seven days a week in his Texas lab with a handful of other enthusiastic scientists, most of whom were also Chinese. (One writer later described the team as "five-sixths Chinese and all work.")

> *We are all friends here. . . . All of us are attracted by Chu's character. The time spent here is very efficient. You feel so satisfied.*
>
> —Ru Ling Meng, scientist in Paul Chu's lab

Chu's lab and another in Tokyo announced in December 1986 that they had duplicated Müller and Bednorz's results. With that, superconductivity research went from almost as cold as the temperatures it required to "red hot." Physicists all over the world began working around the clock to find formulas for other ceramics that could become superconducting at relatively high temperatures. Chu's lab made some of the most daring attempts. "We were willing to try all kinds of . . . experiments to get the temperature higher," he said later. "We . . . believe in wild thinking around here."

Finally, in January 1987, the Texas lab hit pay dirt. The breakthrough compound was a sickly green "ugly duckling" that many labs would have thrown out because only black oxides had been found to conduct electricity. Chu, however, insisted on testing it. The results of a preliminary test "gave us confidence something must be there."

By this time the Texas university had formed a research partnership with the University of Alabama, and Chu was working with Maw-kuen Wu, a Chinese physicist there who had been his student. Chu suggested that Wu test the new ceramic, which contained the rare earth element yttrium in place of the lanthanum that Müller and Bednorz had used. Wu found that it became superconducting at 93° K (–292° F)—warm as a summer day compared with everything that had gone before. "We were so excited and so nervous that our hands were shaking," Wu said later.

Arthur Freeman, a physicist at Northwestern University, later said of this discovery, "A barrier has been broken. It's exciting for the physics community and for mankind as a whole." The new substance was so important because it was the first to become superconducting at a temperature that could be achieved by cooling with liquid nitrogen rather than liquid helium. Liquid nitrogen can be poured

Superconducting materials are repelled by magnets, a phenomenon called the Meissner effect. Here, a pellet of superconducting ceramic similar to those discovered by Paul Chu illustrates this effect by floating above a magnet. Magnets and superconductors can combine to lift trains several inches above the ground, allowing the trains to speed along at 300 miles an hour. (Argonne National Laboratories)

PAUL CHING-WU CHU

from laboratory hoses, stored in thermos bottles, and, one writer said, is "cheaper than Kool-Aid."

Chu and Wu announced their results at the American Physical Society's annual meeting in March 1987. That meeting was even more packed than the meeting of the same group 30 years earlier at which two other Chinese-born physicists, Tsung Dao Lee and Chen Ning Yang, had announced that the law of conservation of parity had been disproved. Indeed, with 3,000 people jamming into a ballroom meant to hold 1,200, the event seemed so much like a rock concert that it became known as "the Woodstock of physics." William Little, a Stanford physicist who attended the meeting, said, "I've never seen anything like it. Physicists are a fairly quiet lot, so to see them elbowing and fighting each other to get into the room was truly remarkable." The party lasted until dawn.

During the spring of 1987, it seemed that higher temperatures for superconductivity were announced by Chu's laboratory or others almost daily. Superconductivity became front-page news, and Chu, the star of the "Woodstock of physics," took on a public appearance schedule as grueling as any rock band's.

The media stories praised the technological miracles that high-temperature superconductivity was supposed to bring. Japan and a few other countries had already built demonstration models of ultrafast "maglev" (magnetic levitation) trains, and the stories predicted that inexpensive magnets made from the new materials would soon make such trains commonplace. Computers with superconducting chips would be faster and more powerful because chip makers could pack circuits closer together without fear of damage from the heat caused by resistance. If electric power were carried through superconducting cables, people would no longer have to pay for the 10 to 20 percent of it that resistance ate up.

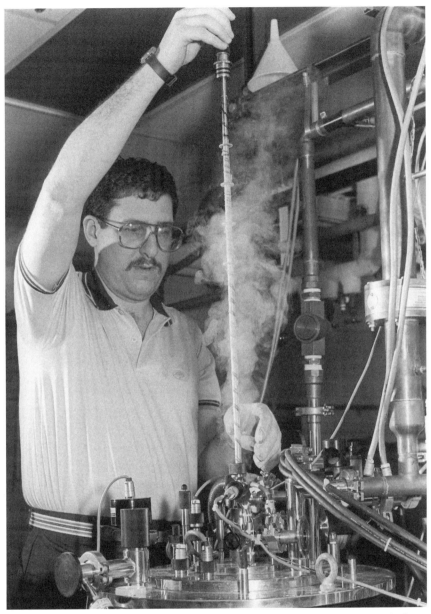

In this photo, taken a few months after Paul Chu announced a breakthrough in high-temperature superconductors, Argonne National Laboratory scientist Don Capone prepares to send a current through a wire made from one of the new superconducting ceramics and cooled to 77° K (−321° F). Argonne was the first American research institution to put current through a wire made from the new superconductors.

(Argonne National Laboratory)

PAUL CHING-WU CHU

Chu and his fellow researchers, however, knew that these dreams were not just around the corner. Many technical problems would have to be solved before the new superconducting materials could be put to practical use. For instance, as anyone who has dropped a pottery dish knows, most ceramics shatter easily. Turning such brittle materials into thin, flexible wires was going to present a real challenge.

In time Paul Chu returned to his lab, but he remained superconductivity's superstar. Late in 1987 the University of Houston made him the director of a new $22.5 million center for superconductivity research, a position he still holds. He won many awards, including the Physical and Mathematical Science Award of the New York Academy of Sciences (1987), the National Medal of Science (1988), and the Comstock Award of the National Academy of Sciences (1988).

Excitement about superconductivity slowly died down as hope and hype gave way to gradual, unspectacular progress. Today, over 100 materials that become superconducting at 134° K (–208° F) or less are known. "It's amazing what has been accomplished in the last 10 years," Chu said in March 1996. The goal of room-temperature superconductivity, however, has yet to be achieved.

Some technical problems have been solved, and some applications of superconductivity have been put into commercial use. For instance, thin films of superconducting material have increased the sensitivity of scientific instruments used to discover defects in materials, prospect for oil, and examine the heart and brain. They may soon filter background noise out of cellular phone base stations and military tracking instruments. The first superconducting underground power cable to be made with a standard industrial process has also been built. The cable, 115 feet (50 meters) long, consists of a hollow tube of liquid nitrogen around which 3.75 miles (6 kilometers) of superconducting ribbon is wrapped.

Many problems still challenge physicists and engineers. Nonetheless, Paul Chu thinks superconductivity technology will have major effects on society. If a room-temperature superconductor is discovered, he says, it "would surely initiate another industrial revolution." Even with just the advances likely to come from existing superconductors, he believes that the "wild thinking" of himself and his fellow researchers will ensure that "the world will never be the same again."

Chronology

1911	Heike Onnes discovers superconductivity
DECEMBER 2, 1941	Ching-wu Chu born in Hunan, China
1968	earns Ph.D. from University of California at San Diego
1979	joins faculty of University of Houston in Texas
1983	Müller and Bednorz begin to test ceramics for superconductivity
JANUARY 27, 1986	discover ceramic that becomes superconducting at −397° F
DECEMBER 1986	Chu duplicates Muller and Bednorz's results
JANUARY 1987	Chu and Maw-kuen Wu discover compound that becomes superconducting at −292° F
MARCH 1987	superconductivity advances announced at "Woodstock of physics"
LATE 1987	Chu made director of new center for superconductivity research in Houston
1997	100 materials that become superconducting at 134° K or less are known; first superconducting power cable built

Further Reading

Chu, Paul C. W. "High-Temperature Superconductors." *Scientific American*, September 1995, pp. 162–165. Describes recent advances in superconductivity technology and predicts future ones.

Gleick, James. "In the Trenches of Science." *New York Times Magazine*, August 16, 1987, pp. 29–30, 55, 74, 77. Describes breakthrough superconductivity research of Paul Chu and others.

Langone, John. *Superconductivity: The New Alchemy*. Chicago: Contemporary Books, 1989. Describes advances in superconductivity research in the 1980s and uses of high-temperature superconductivity.

Lemonick, Michael D. "Superconductors!" *Time*, May 11, 1987, pp. 64–74. Describes exciting possible uses of high-temperature superconductivity.

Maranto, Gina. "Superconductivity: Hype vs. Reality." *Discover*, August 1987, pp. 22–32. Describes possible uses of superconductivity but warns that these may not be practical in the near future.

Reinert, Al. "The Inventive Mr. Chu." *Texas Monthly*, August 1988, pp. 94–96, 140–142. Describes Paul Chu's superconductivity research.

Stwertka, Albert. *Superconductors: The Irresistible Future*. New York: Franklin Watts, 1991. A young adult book on superconductors.

Flossie Wong-Staal

(1946–)

Ten years from now, a woman whose blood carries HIV (human immunodeficiency virus), the virus that causes AIDS, gives birth to a child. A baby born to such a woman today probably would also carry the virus and eventually would develop AIDS. In this future time, however, the baby is injected at birth with genetically engineered blood cells containing a chemical that can destroy the virus. As these cells mature and spread through the child's body, they not only remove the existing virus but give the child a lifelong immunity to the deadly disease.

If this form of gene therapy, or use of altered genes to treat disease, ever becomes a reality, it will be partly because of Chinese-American scientist Flossie Wong-Staal. Wong-Staal has been a leader in research on the AIDS virus since the virus was discovered in 1983. She has also shed light on cancer and the workings of the immune system.

☆ ☆ ☆

Flossie Wong-Staal helped to discover HIV, the virus that causes AIDS, as well as a related virus that causes a rare form of human cancer. She discovered the function of each of HIV's nine genes. Today she is trying to find ways to alter genes to create a vaccine or treatment for AIDS. (Flossie Wong-Staal)

Yee-ching Wong was born on August 27, 1946, in Kuangchou, China, then known to speakers of English as Canton. Her father, Sueh-fung Wong, was a businessman who imported and exported cloth. In 1952, when Yee-ching was five, her family moved to Hong Kong, then a British colony on the south China coast, to escape China's Communist government.

When she was a little older, Yee-ching began attending a girls' school taught by American nuns. They could not pronounce Chinese very well, so they insisted that each student be given an English name. Yee-ching's father decided to choose her name from the newspaper. Tropical storms were given women's names in those days, and a typhoon called Flossie had struck Hong Kong just the week before. The name caught Wong's eye, and so, says Flossie Wong-Staal, "I was named after a typhoon!"

In Hong Kong schools of the time, the teachers decided which course of study each student should follow in high school. They assigned Flossie to the science course. She found that she liked science enough to continue studying it when she entered the University of California at Los Angeles (UCLA) in 1965.

At the time Flossie Wong was in college, scientists like Har Gobind Khorana had just finished cracking the genetic code, and research in molecular biology was advancing rapidly. "It was a very exciting time, and I was just fascinated by it," she recalls. She decided to specialize in this field after graduation. In 1971 she married Steven Staal, a fellow biology student at UCLA. They later had two daughters, Stephanie and Caroline. Wong-Staal, as she now called herself, earned her Ph.D. in 1972, also winning the Woman Graduate of the Year award.

When Steven Staal finished medical school, he chose to do civilian work rather than serve in the Vietnam War. He was assigned to the

Robert Gallo of the National Cancer Institute, part of the National Institutes of Health, was the codiscoverer (with Luc Montagnier of France's Pasteur Institute) of the virus that causes AIDS. He also discovered the first virus shown to cause cancer in humans. He has said that because of her "insight and leadership qualities," Flossie Wong-Staal "evolve[d] into one of the major players" in his laboratory. (National Cancer Institute)

National Institutes of Health (NIH) in Bethesda, Maryland. Wong-Staal also obtained a position at NIH, in the laboratory of Robert Gallo in the National Cancer Institute. She began working there in 1973.

Gallo was doing research on viruses that cause cancer in animals. Other scientists had recently discovered that such viruses did their fatal work by inserting certain genes into cells, making the cells multiply uncontrollably. Even more important, scientists had learned that far back in evolutionary time the viruses had taken these cancer-causing genes, or oncogenes, from cells they infected. Oncogenes were really mutated forms of normal genes that controlled growth. These healthy genes could be converted to a cancer-causing form not only by viruses but by chemicals in the environment and other factors.

In Wong-Staal's first years in Gallo's lab, she studied viruses that cause cancer in monkeys and apes. She looked for oncogenes in the viruses and tried to find genes in human cells that were similar or identical to them. She was the first to locate many of these genes in humans. Some of the genes were also found in a wide variety of animals. This fitted with the idea that in their healthy form, these genes were vital to cells' development.

Gallo was impressed with Wong-Staal's work from the start. He wrote later that she "evolve[d] into one of the major players in my group. Because of her insight and leadership qualities, she gradually assumed a supervisory role." Wong-Staal, in turn, says that Gallo's laboratory "made more original discoveries than any lab I know in biomedical science." She believes that, as Chien-shiung Wu did with Lee and Yang, she made a good working partner for a theorist like Gallo. "He's . . . creative and goes after original observations . . . , while my interest was more analytical," she says.

At the time, no viruses had been proven to cause cancer in humans. Gallo, however, believed that human cancer viruses existed. In 1972 his group had identified in human cancer cells a chemical that was also found in animal cancer viruses. Then, in 1981, they published evidence that a particular virus caused a rare type of human cancer. Gallo called the virus HTLV, or human T-cell leukemia virus, because the cells it made cancerous were the type of white blood cells called T cells. (Susumu Tonegawa had helped to show how these cells function in the immune system.) The group later found a related cancer-causing virus, which they labeled HTLV-2. They and other researchers showed that these viruses could be spread by sexual contact, by transfer of blood (in transfusions or on contaminated hypodermic needles, for instance), and from mother to unborn child. Disease appeared many years after infection with the virus.

At this same time, doctors in a few large cities were noticing a strange cluster of symptoms, or signs of sickness, mostly among homosexual men. These people were weak, thin, and suffering from a variety of unusual illnesses. Some developed a rare cancer that made purple blotches on their skins. Some had pneumonia, a lung disease, caused by a microorganism that healthy immune systems usually destroyed. Doctors slowly realized that all the people's immune systems were severely damaged. By 1983 scientists had given this group of symptoms the name of acquired immunodeficiency syndrome, or AIDS.

At first no one knew what caused AIDS. Gallo and Wong-Staal, however, noticed certain similarities between the new disease and the virus-caused cancer they had been studying. Wong-Staal says:

> I think what struck . . . us . . . is the mode of transmission—it seem[ed] very similar to [that for] the leukemia virus . . . and also the fact that . . . the specific cell that disappears in AIDS is the . . . CD-4 [T] cell, . . . the cell that HTLV transforms [makes cancerous].

It thus seemed possible that HTLV or a related virus caused AIDS.

The researchers found that only about 10 percent of people with AIDS had antibodies to HTLV in their blood, showing that they had been exposed to the virus. All, however, showed antibodies to a similar virus, which Gallo isolated in late 1983 and at first called HTLV-III. At about the

The same virus . . . can induce a cell to grow uncontrollably . . . [or] kill it.

—Flossie Wong-Staal

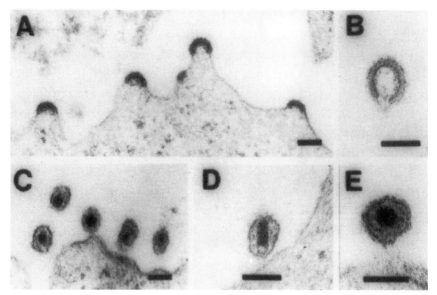

HIV, the AIDS virus, is shown here budding from infected cells. Flossie Wong-Staal is studying a way to damage the virus's genetic material so that it cannot reproduce.
(Reprinted with permission from Jay Levy, "Isolation of Lymphocytopathic Retroviruses from San Francisco Patients with AIDS," *Science*, August 24, 1984. Copyright 1984, American Association for the Advancement of Science.)

same time, researchers at the Pasteur Institute in France, headed by Luc Montagnier, isolated a similar virus. The viruses proved to be identical, and the two laboratories were given joint credit for discovering it, just as Samuel Ting's and Burton Richter's labs had been for finding the J/psi particle. The virus was named HIV (human immunodeficiency virus).

Flossie Wong-Staal used her experimental skills to study the newly identified virus. In 1984 she became the first to clone, or make copies of, the virus's genes. Using genetic engineering techniques, she identified, sequenced, and analyzed each of the nine genes in the HIV genome (complete collection of genes). She found that most of the genes affected the virus's growth. She also showed that some of the genes, like the antibody genes studied by Susumu Tonegawa, changed or mutated easily. This would make developing a vaccine against AIDS difficult because many different variations of the virus were sure to exist.

Wong-Staal's discoveries showed how difficult a task defeating HIV was likely to be, yet they also offered hope. She wrote in 1988, "A molecular description of HIV . . . sets out the vital features of the virus, some of which can serve as the focus of control strategies. Surely this description contains the seeds of HIV's eventual defeat."

Wong-Staal and her husband divorced in 1985, but she continued to use her married name. Her fame in the "hot" field of AIDS research made many universities eager to hire her. In 1990 she decided to go to the University of California at San Diego (UCSD), where she was offered the leadership of a newly established center for AIDS research.

At UCSD, Wong-Staal has turned from basic research on HIV to trying to find ways to defeat the virus through either a vaccine or a treatment. During the early 1990s she tried several approaches to making a vaccine, but these efforts ended in frustration. Her current interest is a combination of treatment and vaccine that involves gene therapy, an infant technology so far used to treat only a few rare diseases.

Wong-Staal and her coworkers have inserted a gene that makes a chemical called a ribozyme into certain harmless viruses. The gene, originally from a virus that infects plants, was altered to act as a "molecular knife" to cut apart HIV's genetic material, which prevents the deadly virus from reproducing. In the laboratory, the ribozyme treatment reduced the quantity of HIV in infected cells by a factor of more than 10,000.

Wong-Staal thinks the treatment may have its greatest use in children born to HIV-infected mothers. Babies' blood contains many immature cells, called stem cells, that will later grow into different types of immune system cells. If some stem cells can be withdrawn before birth, treated with the gene-carrying virus, and then reinjected after a baby is born, Wong-Staal hopes that the cells will be able to destroy not only the HIV that the child got from its mother but any other strain of the virus that it might encounter during its lifetime.

Other scientists greatly respect Wong-Staal's work. One sign of such respect is seen in the number of researchers who cite, or refer to, her papers in the notes of their own research reports. The more important a piece of research is, the more often the paper describing that research is likely to be cited. A study done by the Institute of

Scientific Information in Philadelphia, reported in the magazine *The Scientist* in 1990, claimed that during the 1980s, Wong-Staal's papers had been cited more often than those of any other woman scientist.

Wong-Staal hopes that her studies of HIV will ultimately have effects that reach beyond AIDS. "This epidemic is going to tell us fundamental things about how viruses interact with the immune system," she predicts. Meanwhile, she finds her work very rewarding. "I enjoy discovering new things, finding out new knowledge," she says. "I wouldn't want to do anything else."

Chronology

AUGUST 27, 1946	Yee-ching Wong born in Kuangchou, China
1956	Wong family moves to Hong Kong
1972	Wong-Staal obtains Ph.D. from UCLA
1973	begins work with Robert Gallo at NIH
1981	Gallo's group shows that a virus can cause a human cancer; disease later known as AIDS first described
1983	human immunodeficiency virus (HIV) identified as cause of AIDS
1984	Wong-Staal clones HIV genes
LATE 1980s	identifies, sequences, and analyzes HIV genes

| 1990 | heads Center for AIDS Research at University of California at San Diego; identified as most-cited woman scientist |
| MID-1990s | develops ribozyme treatment for AIDS |

Further Reading

Alvarez, Emilio, and Anne Crystal Angeles. "Science Superstar." *National Geographic World*, June 1993, pp. 26–27. Two teenagers interview Wong-Staal about her AIDS research.

Baskin, Yvonne. "Intimate Enemies." *Discover*, December 1991, pp. 16–17. Article provides background on Wong-Staal and describes her AIDS research in the 1980s.

Gallo, Robert. *Virus Hunting.* New York: New Republic/Basic Books, 1991. Describes Gallo lab's identification of human cancer and AIDS viruses, including Wong-Staal's work. Somewhat difficult reading.

Yount, Lisa. *Contemporary Women Scientists.* New York: Facts On File, 1994. For young people. Includes a chapter on Wong-Staal.

Constance Tom Noguchi has devoted her life to studying red blood cells, which carry oxygen through the body, and to finding treatments for sickle-cell disease, in which a defective gene causes red cells to change shape. (Constance Tom Noguchi)

Constance Tom Noguchi

(1948–)

An African-American woman brings her five-year-old son into a hospital emergency room. The child, small for his age and sickly-looking, is crying in pain. He has an inherited condition called sickle-cell disease, in which an abnormal form of the substance that carries oxygen in his blood makes his red blood cells change shape. These deformed cells, curved like new moons, sometimes block the minute blood vessels in his body. When this happens, his tissues become starved for oxygen. The result is misery.

The emergency room doctors, however, know just what to do. There is no cure for the boy's illness, but a combination of drugs can treat it and take away his pain. This drug combination was developed partly by an Asian-American scientist, Constance Tom Noguchi, who has dedicated her life to improving the health of people with this crippling blood disease.

★ ★ ★

Like Flossie Wong-Staal, Connie Tom came from Kuangchou, or Canton, China. Connie, the third of James and Irene Tom's four daughters, was born there on December 8, 1948. James Tom was a Chinese-American engineer who had been working in China when World War II broke out. He stayed there during the war and married Irene Cheung, a Chinese woman. They had three daughters while still in China. Tom brought his family back to the United States in 1949, when Communists took control of China. They added a fourth daughter in America.

Connie and her sisters grew up in San Francisco, California. The Toms lived on the edge of that city's large Chinese community, and the girls sometimes took part in activities there. The rest of the time, they did the same things as their American schoolmates.

Connie first became interested in science because of the books her father brought home or ordered through the mail. "We had tremendous numbers of books. I think he belonged to almost every book club there was," she recalls.

Science was an exciting subject in school, too. Connie happily remembers one summer during junior high school when she took a special course for students who were interested in science. Each student did a major experiment during the class. "You had to design [the experiment] for yourself and do research on [it in the library] and come up with a rationale for [it] and [describe] what you should expect to see. It was fascinating."

Connie's parents believed strongly in education. "There was never a question that my sisters and I would go to college," she says. "It was just a question of which college." Connie chose the University of California at Berkeley, where her father and two older sisters had studied.

Connie's first plan was to become a physician, or medical doctor, partly because her father wanted a physician in the family. At Berkeley, however, she started to question this choice. For one thing, her introductory courses in biology seemed to consist mostly of memorizing long lists of names and facts rather than doing the sort of independent experimentation she loved. For another, she recalls, "I didn't like the attitudes of my classmates." Most seemed more interested in getting good grades than in thinking for themselves.

One premedical student Connie met was different, however. His name was Phil Noguchi. She married him in 1969, just before the beginning of their senior year. They later had two sons.

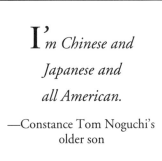

After a few years of studying biology, Connie switched to physics. She liked the way that, at least in theoretical physics, people worked independently with their minds rather than depending on elaborate equipment and a team of other people. Her physics classes seemed "more personal" than the large biology courses she had taken.

Like Chien-shiung Wu, who had also studied at Berkeley, Connie didn't worry that very few other women were interested in physics. That fact combined with her last name to provide some amusing moments in class, however. "When [an] instructor found out that I was Tom, it was sort of a revelation," she chuckles.

Connie Noguchi went to George Washington University in Washington, D.C., for graduate work and obtained her Ph.D. in theoretical nuclear physics in 1975. She had never completely lost her interest in medicine, however, and she decided to use her physics training in the study of disease. Later in 1975 she began research work at the National Institutes of Health (NIH), where Flossie Wong-Staal had also worked for several years. Noguchi is currently chief of the section on Molecular Cell Biology in the Laboratory of Chemical Biology at the National Institute of Diabetes, Digestive and Kidney Diseases at NIH.

The subject Noguchi chose to work on was sickle-cell disease, a common inherited blood disorder found mostly among people of African descent. It is caused by a mutation in a gene that contains part of the orders for making hemoglobin, the iron-containing pigment that carries oxygen through the body and gives blood its red color. As with the antibody molecules that Susumu Tonegawa studied, instructions for making the hemoglobin molecule are carried on several different genes. Hemoglobin genes do not have the tremendous variation that antibody genes do, but several different forms of

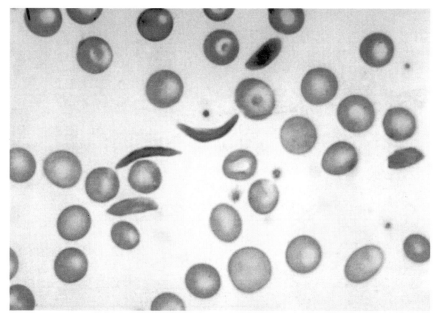

In sickle-cell disease, an abnormal form of hemoglobin, a red pigment that carries oxygen, causes red blood cells like those in the center of this picture to take on a curved or sickled shape. These sickled cells can block tiny blood vessels, depriving the tissues of oxygen. (American Society of Hematology Slide Bank)

hemoglobin do exist. Some are present in a baby's blood before birth, then are mostly replaced by an adult form as the child matures.

The abnormal gene in sickle-cell disease affects the adult form. When hemoglobin made by this gene gives up its oxygen in the body, Noguchi says, it sometimes "becomes . . . like cream cheese. . . . The hemoglobin molecules tend to aggregate [cluster], like pearls on a string." The strings of molecules twist around each other, forming long, ropelike fibers. The fibers bend the red cells until, instead of being round with flat centers—"like a jelly-filled doughnut"—the cells take on the curved form of a crescent moon or the old farm tool called a sickle.

These "sickle-cells" thicken the blood and sometimes clog the body's tiniest blood vessels, the capillaries. When this happens, blood cannot flow into the tissues, and they become starved for oxygen. "Every organ in the body is affected," Noguchi says. The person undergoes a "sickle-cell crisis," producing great pain and, usually, a trip to the hospital. Children with sickle-cell disease tend to be smaller than average and to have poorly functioning immune systems because their bodies are so often short of oxygen. As a result, they suffer frequent infections and may die at an early age.

A child inherits two copies of each of its genes, one from its mother and one from its father. If a child inherits abnormal copies of the gene that causes sickle-cell disease from both parents, it will develop the disease. If the child inherits one abnormal gene and one normal one, however, it will not be sick. Such a person, known as a carrier, will have a fifty-fifty chance of passing on the defective gene to each of his or her offspring. Scientists have found evidence that sickle-cell carriers have some immunity to the most serious form of malaria, a deadly blood disease caused by a parasite that is widespread in Africa. This may explain why the gene for this disease remains so common in certain groups, even though people with two copies of the defective gene seldom live long enough to have children.

Noguchi began her research by studying the way amino acids, building blocks of proteins, behave in sickle-cell hemoglobin. (Hemoglobin is a protein.) She hoped to find a way to keep the hemoglobin molecules from aggregating. Later, Noguchi developed a way to measure the degree to which abnormal hemoglobin forms fibers in the blood cells of a person with sickle-cell disease. This technique has proved useful in evaluating drugs to treat the disease.

Noguchi and other scientists have learned that a drug called hydroxyurea helps some people with sickle-cell disease by increasing the amount of a type of hemoglobin called fetal hemoglobin, which mostly exists before birth but remains in small amounts in adult blood. People with sickle-cell disease who are born with relatively high amounts of fetal hemoglobin in their

I *have . . . enjoyed . . . the ability to do experiments in the lab and to discover the answers. . . . It's . . . fun when they work out the way you expect, but it's even more fun when you get unexpected results.*

—Constance Tom Noguchi

blood have a milder form of the disease. Unlike the defective adult hemoglobin, the fetal hemoglobin in the blood of a person with sickle-cell disease does not make blood cells change shape. Increasing the amount of fetal hemoglobin therefore increases the number of healthy cells. It also seems to make the hemoglobin in the sickled cells less likely to form fibers. Increasing the amount of fetal hemoglobin in a sickle-cell patient's blood is "like doing gene therapy without having to add new genes," Noguchi says.

Noguchi's research has helped to improve the hydroxyurea treatment. For instance, she and her coworkers have found that hydroxyurea works best when combined with other drugs. One drug she has investigated is a hormone called erythropoietin, which helps to produce new red blood cells. When hydroxyurea is combined with small amounts of erythropoietin and an iron supplement, smaller doses of hydroxyurea can be given without losing the drug's helpful effects. High doses of hydroxyurea can damage the body, so the combined treatment is safer than hydroxyurea alone.

As Susumu Tonegawa did with antibodies, Noguchi has also studied the way the several genes involved in hemoglobin production express themselves at different times in life—"the basic mechanism that tells which . . . gene to turn on when." She hopes that this research will eventually lead to better treatments for sickle-cell disease. In addition, she is doing basic research to learn more about erythropoietin and other chemicals and genes involved in the development of normal red blood cells. Noguchi has received several awards for her work, including the Public Health Special Recognition Award (1993) and the NIH EEO Recognition Award (1995).

Connie Noguchi hopes that gene therapy someday can be used to treat sickle-cell disease directly, as Flossie Wong-Staal hopes for AIDS. Noguchi points out that blood diseases, including this one, were among the first inherited conditions considered as possibilities for applying this new form of treatment. The idea of using gene therapy to treat blood diseases was temporarily abandoned, however, because researchers realized that they would have to change most of a person's red cells before they would have much effect on such diseases, and putting new genes into individual cells has been difficult. Gene therapy therefore was tried first in other diseases in which the therapy had a chance of working even if only a small number of cells was changed.

Improvements in methods of inserting genes offer new hope today, Noguchi says. "People are beginning to consider that perhaps gene therapy for sickle-cell disease is not as far down the road."

Chronology

DECEMBER 8, 1948	Constance Tom born in Kuangchou, China
1949	Tom family returns to United States
1975	Connie Noguchi obtains Ph.D. from George Washington University; joins National Institutes of Health
1980s–1990s	does research on hydroxyurea and other treatments for sickle-cell anemia
1990s	studies genes involved in sickle-cell anemia and development of red blood cells
1993	receives the Public Health Special Recognition Award
1995	receives the NIH EEO Recognition Award

Further Reading

Asian-American Biographies. Paramus, N.J.: Globe Fearon, 1994. For young people. Contains a profile of Noguchi.

Verheyden-Hilliard, Mary Ellen. *Scientist and Puzzle Solver, Constance Tom Noguchi.* Bethesda, Md.: Equity Institute, 1985. For young readers.

David Ho made basic discoveries about how the AIDS virus reproduces during the course of the disease. He has helped to develop a new combination drug treatment that is prolonging the lives of people with AIDS, and his recommendation that the treatment be begun soon after infection may lead to the first cures for the disease. (photo Bob Reichert; Aaron Diamond AIDS Research Center)

David Da-i Ho

(1952–)

In mid-1995, 37-year-old Dan Cusick of San Francisco was told he had only a few months to live. Cusick's immune system had been almost completely destroyed by AIDS, and an infection was attacking his brain. His desperate doctors then tried a new approach: giving him a combination of drugs that targets HIV, the virus that causes the disease, at several different points in its life cycle. The infection began to clear up within weeks. Shortly afterward, HIV could no longer be found in his blood.

Linda Grinberg of Brentwood, California, who also has AIDS, could hardly dress herself. Like Cusick, she did not expect to live out the year. Her doctors gave her a drug mixture similar to the one that saved Cusick. A year and a half later, she said, "It's given me back my life."

Neither Cusick nor Grinberg is cured of AIDS. For the first time, however, they and others like them have a reasonable chance of survival. The hope is even greater for people who begin taking the "drug cocktail" soon after their infection by HIV, when their immune systems are still relatively healthy. This new hope is the result of work by many scientists, but one of the chief ones is a Chinese American named David Ho. Because of Ho's contributions to AIDS research, *Time* magazine named him Man of the Year in 1996.

☆ ☆ ☆

Da-i Ho was born on November 3, 1952, in Taichung, Taiwan. His name means "Great One." Hoping to provide a better life for his family than he could do in Taiwan, Da-i's father, an engineer and computer scientist, moved to the United States in 1956. For nine years, Da-i and his younger brother heard from him only by letter.

In 1965, when Da-i was twelve, the rest of the Ho family at last moved to Los Angeles to join the father. He had chosen the Biblical name Paul for himself in the new country, and he now picked names from the Bible for his sons as well. Da-i became David, and his brother became Phillip. Their mother chose the name Sonia. Later a third son was born to the family, and David and Phillip were allowed to choose their new brother's name. They picked Sidney—not from the Bible but from a Jerry Lewis movie.

While Paul Ho completed his master's degree in engineering at the University of Southern California, his sons struggled to learn English. Ho had forbidden them to study the language in Taiwan because he wanted them to speak it without an accent. "We hadn't even learned the ABC's," David Ho recalls. "I remember being laughed at by classmates who thought I was dumb." They changed their minds when they found that he was years ahead of them in math.

David Ho went to college at Caltech. Like Connie Noguchi, he changed majors as an undergraduate, but he went in the opposite direction: Whereas Noguchi had changed from a premedical course to physics, Ho switched from physics to premedicine. Physics had felt more "personal" than biology to Noguchi, but it seemed too abstract for Ho. The results of the changes were similar, however. In the end, Ho became fascinated by molecular biology, just as Noguchi and Flossie Wong-Staal had. He graduated summa cum laude in 1974, then went to medical school at Harvard and earned his M.D. in 1979.

While Ho was still at Caltech, friends introduced him to an artist named Susan Kuo. She studied at the Boston Museum of Fine Arts while he was at Harvard. They married and had three children, Kathryn, Jonathan, and Jaclyn.

During his second year as a doctor, Ho worked at Cedars Sinai Hospital in Los Angeles. He began seeing patients, mostly gay men, who suffered from weakness and rare infections. Another Los Angeles doctor, Michael Gottlieb, wrote a medical article at about this same time that described a group of similar people. Gottlieb's patients were the first to be identified with the set of symptoms that soon would be known as AIDS. Ho, who met two of the five people Gottlieb wrote about, was one of the first doctors to suspect that their illness was caused by an infectious microorganism, probably a virus.

He's kind of a genius, you know. I'm not supposed to say that, but it's true.

—Sonia Ho,
David Ho's mother

Like Flossie Wong-Staal, Ho decided to study the new illness. In 1982 he moved to the laboratory of Martin Hirsch at Massachusetts General Hospital in Boston, which specialized in the study of viruses. There he and his coworkers made several important discoveries about AIDS and the virus that caused it. They were the fourth group in the world to isolate HIV, and they were the first to locate it in a type of immune system cells called macrophages. They were among the first to find it in men's semen and in cells of the nervous system. On the other hand, they showed that there was not enough virus in saliva to transmit the infection. This fact reassured people that they could not catch AIDS from, say, sharing a drinking glass with someone who had the disease. "David had the Midas touch," Hirsch remembers. "Whatever he did worked."

To earn extra money to support his growing family, Ho also worked at a clinic in the hospital. There he frequently saw young gay men who seemed to have severe cases of flu. Ho wondered if this illness might be the first sign of infection by HIV. Sure enough, tests of the men's blood revealed HIV rather than flu virus. A few weeks later, as the "flu" died down, antibodies to the virus appeared in the men's blood, and the virus itself seemingly vanished. Ho had found the first evidence that HIV caused an active infection right after it entered people's bodies.

In the mid-1980s, Ho and his family moved back to California. He joined the faculty of UCLA and continued his AIDS research. Using a new test that could show the amount of virus in a person's blood, he discovered, to his surprise, that people in the first stages of HIV infection had as high a level of virus as people with fully developed AIDS. He and another group of researchers headed by George Shaw, who had made the same discovery independently, reported it jointly in 1991.

In that same year, Ho was chosen to head the Aaron Diamond Center for AIDS Research, which had just opened in New York City. Ho was only 37 years old and relatively unknown at the time, but Irene Diamond, who provided much of the money for the center, said later, "I [didn't] want a star, I want[ed] a wonderful scientist." Ho still directs the center, which is now one of the largest AIDS research centers in the world.

The first drug used to treat AIDS was AZT, or zidovudine, which blocks a chemical needed in an early stage of HIV's reproduction. It was first approved for use by the Food and Drug Administration (FDA) in 1987. AZT was better than nothing, but it could have severe side effects, and it helped only some patients. Worst of all, it often became ineffective even in people it had helped because some of the viruses in their bodies mutated and developed resistance to it.

For several years there seemed to be no answer to this problem. Then, during the mid-1990s, several additional drugs that attacked HIV were developed. One, 3TC, worked similarly to AZT but often was effective in people whose virus had become resistant to the older drug. Other drugs, called protease inhibitors, destroyed the virus in a totally different way, blocking a later stage in its reproduction. David Ho was one of several scientists who suggested that people with AIDS be given all three types of drug at once. That lessened the chance that resistant viruses could escape the drugs and multiply.

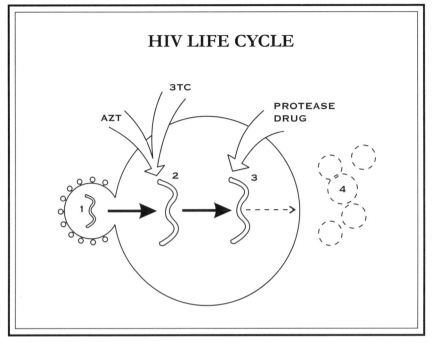

HIV LIFE CYCLE

Drugs in the combination treatment recommended by David Ho attack HIV at several different points in its life cycle, shown here. At (1) the virus enters a cell. AZT and 3TC disrupt the virus's reproduction at an early stage (2) by blocking a chemical that changes the virus's genetic material into a form that the cell can be forced to copy. Protease inhibitors block a later stage (3), in which proteins made by the cell at the virus's orders are cut into pieces that can be incorporated into new viruses. As a result, no new viruses are produced (4). (Katherine Macfarlane)

Meanwhile, Ho made some basic discoveries about how HIV works that would bring even greater hope to some people infected with the virus. Scientists had thought that HIV hid quietly in immune system cells, seldom reproducing, for three to 10 years after infection before beginning to multiply rapidly again and producing full-blown AIDS. Ho and George Shaw, however, began to doubt whether this was so. If the virus was creating many copies of itself, but the immune system was destroying them as fast as they were produced, low levels of virus would appear in the blood, just as if the virus were hardly reproducing at all. Ho compares the situation to that of a person running on a treadmill: No matter how fast the person goes, he or she will seem to stay in the same place. Only when

The development of AIDS can be likened to an impending [oncoming] train wreck, where the viral load [amount of virus in the blood] indicates the speed with which the train is headed for catastrophe and the CD4 [T] cell count marks the distance from the site of doom.

—David Ho

the immune system became exhausted would the levels of detectable virus rise.

To find out how fast HIV was really reproducing, the researchers would have to stop the treadmill. If the virus was reproducing rapidly and they blocked it temporarily, the number of healthy T cells, the chief kind of immune cell that the virus attacks, should rise very quickly. If the virus was reproducing slowly, however, reducing its reproduction rate a little further should not have much effect. Ho and Shaw decided to try the effect of the new protease inhibitors, which cut off reproduction of HIV almost completely at least for a while.

Ho's and Shaw's competing laboratories began their experiments at about the same time. Ho made his test on 20 volunteers who had fewer than 500 T cells per milliliter of blood, less than half the normal amount. When these people were given a protease inhibitor, the number of viruses in their blood dropped to almost zero, and their T cell levels rose rapidly. Shaw's group got similar results. By 1995 the two scientists had concluded that, even during the supposedly quiet period in which people with HIV infections seemed healthy, the virus was producing billions of copies of itself each day. The immune system, in turn, sacrificed billions of cells to destroy them. Over the ten years AIDS normally took to develop, a total of some 10 trillion viruses and cells might be produced. As *Time* reporter Christine Gorman wrote, "The wonder was not that the immune system eventually crashed. Given such intense fighting and heavy casualties, the wonder was that it lasted so long."

Doctors normally gave the new "cocktail" of AZT, 3TC, and protease inhibitors only to people who were already seriously ill with

AIDS. This seemed to make sense because all the drugs could have severe side effects, and all were expensive. If the virus was fairly inactive before full-blown AIDS set in, there was little point in treating it during that time. Ho and Shaw's research, however, showed that the virus was never inactive.

Furthermore, Ho found in 1995 that right after infection, all the AIDS viruses in a person's body were similar. Each time the viruses reproduced, however, they had a chance to mutate. The more mutations they underwent, the greater the chances became that some of the viruses would be resistant to one or more drugs. If the viruses reproduced rapidly throughout the course of infection, it made sense to try to destroy them as soon as possible, before they had time to diversify and develop resistance. Ho therefore recommended "hit[ting] HIV early and hard" with the combination treatment, giving the drugs as soon as HIV infection was detected.

Ho and researcher Martin Markowitz tried this approach on 24 men in a very early stage of HIV infection. After more than a year of treatment, there was no sign of the virus in the men's blood, although the researchers suspected that some virus particles were hiding out elsewhere in their bodies. Mathematical models predict that the drugs could get rid of all the virus in two to three years. One of the men has agreed that, if no virus can be found in his body at that time, he will stop taking the drugs and wait to see whether the virus returns. If it does not, he will be the first person considered cured of AIDS.

Ho reported his hopeful results in July 1996 at the 11th International Conference on AIDS in Vancouver, Canada. According to *Time* magazine, Ho's report "provided concrete evidence that HIV is not insurmountable." If a cure for AIDS does develop from these experiments, millions of people will largely have David Ho to thank.

Chronology

NOVEMBER 3, 1952	Da-i Ho born in Taichung, Taiwan
1965	Ho family moves to United States

1979	Ho obtains M.D. degree from Harvard
1981	treats some of first patients identified with AIDS
1982	moves to Massachusetts General Hospital
EARLY 1980S	finds HIV in macrophages, semen, nerve cells; identifies earliest stage of HIV infection
1987	AZT approved for treating AIDS
1991	Ho and Shaw discover high levels of virus in blood in early stages of HIV infection; Ho becomes head of Aaron Diamond Center for AIDS Research
MID-1990S	3TC, protease inhibitors used to treat AIDS; Ho recommends using these drugs with AZT
1995	Ho and Shaw show that HIV reproduces rapidly even during "quiet" period of infection; Ho recommends using drug combination early in infection
JULY 1996	reports that early drug treatment has eliminated HIV from blood of some patients

Further Reading

Chua-eoan, Howard. "The Tao of Ho." *Time*, December 30, 1996–January 6, 1997, pp. 69–70. Describes Ho's family background and childhood.

Gorman, Christine. "A New Attack on AIDS." *Time*, July 8, 1996, pp. 52–53. Describes success of multidrug therapy for AIDS, including Ho's contribution.

Ho, David D. "Time to Hit HIV, Early and Hard." *New England Journal of Medicine*, August 17, 1995, pp. 450–451. Explains why Ho believes patients should be given multiple drugs as soon as possible after HIV infection. Difficult reading.

Park, Alice, and Dick Thompson. "The Disease Detective." *Time*, December 30, 1996–January 6, 1997, pp. 56–62. Describes AIDS research that made *Time* name Ho its "Man of the Year."

Ragaza, Angelo. *Lives of Notable Asian Americans.* New York: Chelsea House, 1995. For young adults. Includes good chapter on Ho.

Richardson, Sarah. "The Race Against AIDS." *Discover*, May 1995, pp. 28, 32. Describes Ho's discovery that HIV multiplies rapidly during "quiet" stage of infection and his recommendation of early drug treatment.

Tsutomu Shimomura

(1964–)

Today, a world of information lies at the fingertips of anyone with a computer, a telephone line, and a connecting device called a modem. Through these devices and associated software (computer programs), people can find out about jobs, take classes, and make arrangements for vacations. They can become friends with people whom they never see face-to-face. It's no wonder that the Internet, the invisible web of computer and telephone links that makes this exchange of information possible, has been called the "information superhighway."

Unfortunately, the information superhighway has its carjackers. Instead of guns, they use sophisticated technical knowledge and clever acting to trick machines and people into giving them information to which they have no right. Some use the information for financial gain or to cause damage that can cost individuals or companies millions of dollars.

Japanese-American scientist Tsutomu Shimomura is an expert on the information superhighway and the computers that power it. He has used computers to investigate the physical world. He has also developed techniques to discover and repair communication weaknesses that threaten the privacy of computer users, and he has helped to track down people who invade that privacy.

☆ ☆ ☆

Tsutomu Shimomura, like Susumu Tonegawa, came from Nagoya, Japan. Shimomura was born there on October 23, 1964. His father, Osamu, was a biochemist, and Akemi, his mother, was a pharmacologist, or scientist who studies drugs. "Being raised by two scientists unquestionably shaped my approach to the world," Shimomura has written. "I was encouraged to ask questions. . . . My parents' response was often to suggest an experiment through which I could determine the answer for myself."

In Tsutomu's earliest years, his parents did research in both Japan and the United States. By the time he started kindergarten, however, they had settled permanently at Princeton University in New Jersey. Torn between two languages and cultures, Tsutomu wrote later that he "never really felt that [he] fit in" in either Japan or America.

He did fit into the fast-growing world of computers, however. He saw his first computer when he was in kindergarten and joined a teenage computer club at the age of 10. Most computers at that time were minicomputers, smaller than the room-sized mainframes of the 1950s but not yet as small or easy to use as the popular personal computers that would develop during the later 1970s.

Tsutomu skipped two grades and began high school at the age of 12. Even so, his classes bored him. He spent most of his time at the university, where, for instance, he became the astronomy department's "computing wizard" when he was just 14. His programming skills let him "work with a lot of very bright people who were doing what they loved, and gave me access to some of the world's best toys." He met more bright people and learned more about their "toys" by exploring the ancestor to the Internet, a Pentagon-funded computer communications network called ARPAnet.

Tsutomu was expelled from high school because of "uninspiring" grades and a reputation for pranks. Even so, good college board scores and recommendations from friends at Princeton gained him admission to Caltech in 1982. By this time he was sure he wanted to study science.

At Caltech, Shimomura repeated his pattern from high school: ignoring regular classes while doing graduate-level work with scientists and subjects that interested him. He left the university in 1984, when Los Alamos National Laboratories in New Mexico offered him a postdoctoral fellowship—in spite of the fact that he was just 19 years old and had graduated from neither high school nor college.

While at Los Alamos, Shimomura created, among other things, computer models that showed how molecules move in fluids. The lab's government bureaucracy irritated him, however, and he was happy to leave in 1988 and join the physics department at the University of California at San Diego, the university where Flossie Wong-Staal works.

In the early 1990s, as a senior fellow at the university's new Supercomputer Center, Shimomura spent some of his time constructing computer models of complex physical phenomena. The rest was devoted to discovering and mending design flaws that let unauthorized people tamper with the computer systems on which government and business increasingly depended.

One computer security investigation brought Tsutomu Shimomura national fame. On the day after Christmas in 1994, he was on his way to a skiing vacation at Lake Tahoe when his assistant, Andrew Gross, called him on his cellular telephone. Gross reported that someone had electronically broken into Shimomura's complex computer system.

Shimomura was both angry and worried. Some information stored on his system, such as a program that allowed people to use cellular telephones to eavesdrop on others' conversations, could be dangerous in the wrong hands. He told Gross to "freeze" the system to preserve any traces of the intruder, much as police might block off a crime scene to protect evidence left there, and then unhappily returned to San Diego.

When he got back, another nasty surprise was waiting: a message on his voice mail spoken in a fake British accent. "My technique is the best," the voice said. "Don't you know who I am? Me and my friends, we'll kill you." Shimomura assumed that the message was a taunt from the person who had invaded his system.

Shimomura went over the records of transactions on his computers with the care of a detective searching for microscopic clues. By New Year's Day of 1995 this technique revealed how the intruder had gained entrance. By sending false signals, the invader had convinced a computer in Shimomura's system that it was communicating with another computer on the same system. The two computers "trusted" each other and accepted each other's inputs without question. The intruder then inserted a program into the second computer that, in turn, allowed access to a third computer in the system. From this computer the cyberburglar copied a variety of Shimomura's files, including his private electronic mail and the cellular telephone software. The method that the computer thief used is called IP spoofing. It had been known as a possibility for over 10 years, but as far as Shimomura knew, no one had actually employed it before.

Shimomura told several friends about his break-in and found that some of their systems had been invaded, too. One friend, Mark Lottor, thought his own break-in might have been done by Kevin Mitnick, a well-known member of the computer underground. The 31-year-old Mitnick had been arrested five times and had served about a year in jail for theft of valuable programs. Since 1992 he had been in hiding, wanted by the FBI for violating the terms of his probation. Media stories called him the country's most wanted computer criminal. Shimomura began to wonder whether Mitnick was responsible for his break-in.

In addition to taking steps to protect his own system, Shimomura wanted to warn other computer users about the new break-in technique. Among other things, he spoke to John Markoff, a *New York Times* reporter in San Francisco who had worked with him on an earlier computer security case. On

> I*n my estimation [Shimomura] is the brightest in security on the whole Internet. . . . I have a lot of respect for this guy.*
>
> —Kevin Mitnick

January 22 Markoff published an article about Shimomura's break-in, claiming:

> The new form of attack leaves many of the 20 million government, business, university and home computers on the global Internet vulnerable to eavesdropping and theft. . . . The problem [of the new technique] is akin to homeowners discovering that burglars have master keys to all the front doors in the neighborhood.

In a follow-up article, Markoff said that Shimomura "considers solving the crime a matter of honor."

On January 27 the case took a new turn when Bruce Koball, a Berkeley, California, software designer who used a computer communications network called the WELL (Whole Earth 'Lectronic Link), made a startling discovery. WELL staff members had puzzled Koball by complaining about several large data files stored in one of his accounts. Koball examined the files and found that some contained mail messages with Shimomura's name on them. He alerted Shimomura that someone had tried to hide material belonging to him on the WELL.

Eager to find the person who had broken into their system, WELL administrators agreed to work with Shimomura and the FBI. Shimomura arrived in Sausalito, the beachfront town near San Francisco where the WELL's headquarters were located, on February 8.

Examination of suspicious WELL accounts turned up more stolen files, including more than 20,000 credit card numbers and computer passwords belonging to subscribers of another Internet service provider, Netcom. After tracking activity in the tampered accounts, Shimomura concluded that only one person was intruding and that the person was probably in the Midwest or the East. The intruder apparently was communicating with the computers through a cellular telephone, an unusual approach because cell phone connections are often too unreliable for data transmission.

Shimomura also began observing certain accounts at Netcom, especially one called *gkremen*. Focusing on this account, he and the other investigators were soon able to watch the intruder's sessions on the network as they occurred. The group saw him read people's electronic mail and chat with a fellow member of the computer underground in Israel, for instance. Shimomura found that most *gkremen* calls could be traced either to Denver, Colorado, or to Raleigh, North Carolina.

In one talk between their intruder and the Israeli, the investigators finally got proof that the person they were monitoring was Kevin Mitnick. The intruder typed, "Markoff . . . is the reason why my picture was [on] the front page of the new york times." Markoff had written a front-page article about Mitnick on July 4, 1994, but he had never featured any other computer criminal in this way. In the same conversation, the intruder referred slightingly to "Japboy," presumably meaning Shimomura. This fit with some later messages that Shimomura had gotten on his voice mail, in which the speaker seemed to mock Shimomura's Japanese heritage by imitating the style of dialogue in kung fu movies.

Now Shimomura began working with FBI and telephone company experts to find out precisely where Mitnick was. They narrowed the possibilities down to a small area in Raleigh. Shimomura flew to Raleigh on February 12 . Using an antenna and other equipment that could home in on Mitnick's phone signals, FBI agents and engineers from the Sprint cellular phone system, with Shimomura in tow, tracked the fugitive to an apartment complex called the Player's Club.

At 2 A.M. on February 15, while Shimomura waited outside, two FBI agents carrying a warrant and a hand-held signal strength meter entered the Player's Club. Mitnick, as usual, was on the phone, and the agents followed his cellular signal to Apartment 202. Ironically, the phone call that gave him away was not made to a computer or another member of the underground. When the agents knocked on his door to arrest him, Kevin Mitnick was chatting with his mother in Las Vegas.

Later that day, Mitnick was arraigned on 23 counts of computer fraud. At his hearing, he and Tsutomu Shimomura met face-to-face for the first time. Shimomura says that when Mitnick recognized him, he said, "Tsutomo, I respect your skills."

A final irony remained. Eight hours after Mitnick was arrested, the same person who had taunted Shimomura on Christmas Day left him another message. The message could not have come from Mitnick, so it appeared that someone else must also have been involved in the break-in. No one knows who this other person was.

If convicted on all the charges against him and given the maximum term for each, Mitnick could have been sentenced to 460 years in jail. In fact, however, all but one of the charges were eventually dropped, and Mitnick plea-bargained on that one to receive jail time of only eight months.

Computer security is full of tradeoffs. The art form is coming up with a set of tradeoffs you can live with.

—Tsutomu Shimomura

In a way, Mitnick's activities did the Internet's estimated 20 million users a favor. The wide publicity given his case made people and companies aware, in some cases for the first time, that, as reporter Jonathan Littman puts it, "The Internet is about as safe as a convenience store in East L.A. on Saturday night." Some people have responded to this threat by calling for stiffer laws against computer crime. Shimomura, however, says that the best ways to stop computer theft and invasion of privacy are to be aware of the danger and to use encryption or coding programs so that data, even if taken, cannot be interpreted by outsiders.

Defenders of Mitnick have pointed out that he caused no damage and did not use his stolen information for profit. Nonetheless, Shimomura feels that Mitnick and others like him have done real harm by destroying the openness that once marked the Internet. He writes:

> The network of computers known as the Internet began as a unique experiment in building a community of people who shared a set of values about technology. . . . That community was based largely on . . . trust. Today, the electronic walls going up everywhere on the Net are the clearest proof of the loss of that trust and community.

Tsutomo Shimomura has vowed to use all his computer skills to keep this loss from growing.

Chronology

OCTOBER 23, 1964	Tsutomu Shimomura born in Nagoya, Japan
1969	Shimomura family moves to United States
1978	Shimomura becomes Princeton astronomy department's "computing wizard" at age 14
1984	leaves Caltech without graduating; begins working for Los Alamos National Laboratories
1988	moves to University of California at San Diego
1992	Kevin Mitnick becomes a fugitive
DECEMBER 26, 1994	Shimomura learns of computer system break-in
JANUARY 1, 1995	figures out break-in method used by intruder
JANUARY 27	Shimomura's files discovered on the WELL
FEBRUARY 8	Shimomura begins investigating at the WELL
FEBRUARY 12	follows Mitnick's trail to Raleigh, North Carolina
FEBRUARY 15	FBI arrests Mitnick

Further Reading

Goodell, Jeff. "The Samurai and the Cyberthief." *Rolling Stone*, May 4, 1995. Concise description of Shimomura's tracking of Kevin Mitnick.

Littman, Jonathan. *The Fugitive Game.* Boston: Little, Brown, 1996. Describes pursuit of Mitnick from Mitnick's point of view, based on electronic conversations; critical of Shimomura and Markoff.

Meyer, Michael, "Stop! Cyberthief!" *Newsweek*, February 6, 1995, pp. 36–39. Describes dangers from criminals on the Internet; mentions break-in of Shimomura's computer system.

Shimomura, Tsutomu, with John Markoff. *Takedown.* New York: Hyperion, 1996. Shimomura's account of pursuit and capture of Kevin Mitnick; includes information about Shimomura's earlier life.

Sussman, Vic. "Policing Cyberspace." *U.S. News and World Report*, January 23, 1995, pp. 55–60. Describes dangers to free Internet communication from cybercriminals and from those trying to capture them.

Index

Boldface numbers indicate main topics. *Italic* page numbers indicate illustrations or captions.

B cells 47, 50
Bednorz, Georg 59–60
behavior, effect of genes on 53
Beijing 14
Bennett, J. C. 47–50
Berkeley, University of California at 16, 19, 78, 79
beryllium 37
beta particles 19, *20*, 21
Big Bang 42
black hole 1–2, 7
blood
  cells 47, *48, 67, 80*
  diseases 82
Boston Museum of Fine Arts 87
Brack, Christine 51
Brahman caste xi
Brentwood (California) 85
Britain xi, 2–5, 7, 27, 68, 97
British Columbia, University of 28
Brookhaven National Laboratory 37, *38*

C

California Institute of Technology (Caltech) 17, 47, 51, 86, 87, 97
California, University of
  Berkeley 16, 19, 78, 79
  Los Angeles 69, 88
  San Diego 47, 57, 73, 97
Cambridge University (Britain) 2, 4–5, 7, 27

cancer 67–71
Canton (China) 68, 78
capillaries 80
Capone, Don 63
CD4 cells *see* T cells
Cedars Sinai Hospital 87
cellular telephones
  security 97–100
  superconductivity effect on 55, 64
ceramics, superconducting 59–60, *61, 63,* 64
CERN (European Organization for Nuclear Research) 36, 41
Chandrasekhar, Subrahmanyan x–xiii, *xvi*, **1–11**, 15, 22, 27
  childhood and education 2, 4
  chronology 10–11
  further reading 11
  Nobel Prize and other awards 7, 9
  research 6
  star life cycle, research on *xvi*, 1, 4–7
  work style 5–6, 9
Chandrasekhar limit 7
charm quark 39, 41
Cheng-Kung University 57
Cheung, Irene 78
Chicago, University of 5, 10, 15, 16
Chin, Jeannette Hui-chung 16
China ix, x, xi, 14, 15, 16, 18, 36, 57, 68, 78, 86
Chu, Paul Ching-wu xii, **55–66,** 56

awards 64
  childhood and education 57
  chronology 65
  further reading 66
  superconductivity research 59–65
Cleveland (Ohio) State University 59
cobalt-60 19, *20,* 21
Cohen, Marvin 62
Columbia University 16, 18, 19, 21, 22, 30, 36
Communists 36, 68, 78
computers
  communication 95–96, 98, 101–103
  security 95–103
  superconductivity effect on 55, 56, 62
conductors, electrical 57, *58*
constant region (of antibodies) 48, *49,* 50
copper 59
Cornell University 30
cosmic rays 42
Crab Nebula *8*
Crease, Robert 41
Crick, Francis 25, 27–28
Cusick, Dan 85
cyclotrons 16, 19 *See also* atom smashers
cytoplasm *29*
cytosine 27–28

D

"dark" matter 43
Denver 100

Massachusetts Institute of Technology (MIT) 30, 36, 52

Matthias, Bernd 57, 59

Meng, Ru Ling 60

messenger RNA (mRNA) 28, *29*, 30

metals 57, 59

Michigan, University of 36

Meissner effect *61*

Milky Way 6, 7, 42

Mitnick, Kevin 98, 100–103

modem 95

molecular biology xi, xii, 45, 47, 51, 69, 86

Montagnier, Luc 69, 72

mRNA *See* messenger RNA

Müller, Karl Alex 59–60

N

Nagoya (Japan) 47, 96

NASA (National Aeronautics and Space Administration) 42

National Academy of Sciences (U.S.) 29, 64

National Bureau of Standards 19

National Cancer Institute (at NIH) 69–70

National Central University (China) 19

National Institute of Diabetes, Digestive, and Kidney Diseases (at NIH) 79

National Institutes of Health (NIH) 30, 69, 70, 79, 82

National Medal of Science (U.S.) 9, 22, 64

National Southeast Associated University (China) 15

Netcom 99

neutron star 7

Newton, Sir Isaac 9

New York Times 98, 100

NIH *See* National Institutes of Health

Nirenberg, Marshall 30

nitrogen, liquid 60, 62, 64

Nobel Prize xi, xiii, 2, 7, 9, 21, 22, 23, 30, 41, 52

Noguchi, Constance Tom ix–xii, **76–83**, 76, 86
  awards 82
  childhood and education 78–79
  chronology 83
  further reading 83
  hemoglobin gene research 82
  sickle-cell disease research 76–77, 79–82

Noguchi, Phil x, 79

Northwestern University 60

nucleic acids *See* DNA; RNA

O

oncogenes 70

Onnes, Heike 57

organ transplants, immune attack on 53

oxides 59, 60

oxygen 47, 48, 59, 76, 77, 79–81

P

Pakistan 2, 27

Palo Alto (California) 39, 40

parity, law of conservation of 14, 16–22, 39, 59, 62

Parker, Eugene N. 10

Pasteur Institute *69*, 72

Pentagon 96

phenylalanine 30

Physics Today 9

pi mesons (pions) 16

plasma 6

positrons 37, 39, 41

Presidency College (India) 2, 5

Princeton University 16, 19, 22, 96

Principia Mathematica 9

protease inhibitors 88–90, *89*

proteins 28–30, *29*, 47, 49, 51, 52, 81, 89

protons 15, 37

psi particle *see* J/psi particle

Punjab (India) 27

Punjab University 27

Q

quarks 39, 41

R

Rabi, I. I. 21
Rai, Ganpat 27
Raipur (India) 27
Raleigh (North Carolina) 100
Raman, Chandrasekhara Venkata 2
Ramanujan, Srinivasa 2
red blood cells 47, *48*, 76–77, 80, 82–83
relativity 4
resistance, drug 91
resistance, electrical 56, 57, *58*, 62
ribonucleic acid *See* RNA
ribosomes 28, 29, 30
ribozyme 73
Richter, Burton 39, 40, 41, 72
RNA (ribonucleic acid) 27–32
  messenger (mRNA) 28–30, *29*
  proteins, making 28–30, *29*
  transfer (tRNA) 28–32, *29*
rotational momentum 39
Royal Astronomical Society 4, 9
Royal Society 2, 9

S

Salamon, Michael 42
saliva, HIV in 87
San Diego, University of California at 47, 57, 73, 97
San Francisco 78, 85, 98–99
Sausalito (California) 99
Science News 41
Scientific American 9, 50
Scientist, The 74
Segré, Emilio 22
semen, HIV in 87
serine 29
Shanghai 15
Shaw, George 88, 89
Shimomura, Akemi 96
Shimomura, Osamu 96
Shimomura, Tsutomo ix–xii, **95–103**
  childhood and education 96–97
  chronology 102
  computer security investigations 95–103
  further reading 103
  research 97
Sibler, Esther Elizabeth 28
sickle-cell disease 22, 76–77, 79–83, *80*
Smith College 19
Society of English Scientists 41
Southern California, University of (USC) 86
Sprint cellular phone system 100
Staal, Steven 69, 73
Stanford Linear Accelerator (SLAC) 39, 40
stars
  clusters 6
  energy transfer in 6
  life cycle xvi, 1, 4–8

mass, effect on life cycle 4, 7–8
  neutron 7
  radiation 6
State University of New York at Stony Brook 22
stem cells 73
Struve, Otto 5
subatomic particles 15–17, 19, 34, 35, 38, 41, 57 *See also names of specific kinds*
  antimatter particles 35, 37, 41–43
  decay of 16, 19, 20, 43
  parity conservation law and 16–17, 19–22
superconductivity 55–66, 58, 61
  defined 55–58, *58*
  high-temperature 59–60, 62–66
  uses of 55, 56, 58, 61, 62, 64, 66
supernova explosion 1, 7, *8*
Switzerland 36, 47, 59

T

Tahoe, Lake 97
Taichung (Taiwan) 86
Taipei 36
Taiwan x, 36, 57, 86
Tamil (language) 2
tau-theta puzzle 16–17
3TC 88–90, *89*
T cells 52, 70–71, 90
telephones, cellular *See* cellular telephones
Teller, Edward 15